Raw for Dessert

EASY DELIGHTS FOR EVERYONE

Jennifer Cornbleet

BOOK PUBLISHING COMPANY

Summertown, Tennessee

Library of Congress Cataloging-in-Publication Data

Cornbleet, Jennifer, 1972-
 Raw for dessert : easy delights for everyone / by Jennifer Cornbleet.
  p. cm.
 Includes index.
 ISBN 978-1-57067-236-1
1. Desserts. 2. Cookery (Natural foods) 3. Raw foods. I. Title.
 TX773.C63443 2009
 641.8'6—dc22

                                        2009020653

Cover and interior design: *Aerocraft Charter Art Service*
Cover and interior photos: *Warren Jefferson*
Food styling: *Barbara Jefferson, Jennifer Cornbleet*

Printed in Canada

Book Publishing Company
P.O. Box 99
Summertown, TN 38483
888-260-8458
www.bookpubco.com

ISBN-13 978-1-57067-236-1

17 16 15 14 13 12 11   3 4 5 6 7 8 9

Book Publishing Co. is a member of Green Press Initiative.
We chose to print this title on paper with postconsumer
recycled content, processed without chlorine, which saved
the following natural resources:

41 trees

1.754 pounds of solid waste

15, 039 gallons of wastewater

3,325 pounds of greenhouse gases

29 million BTU of total energy

For more information, visit www.greenpressinitiative.org.

Paper calculations from Environmental Defense Paper Calculator,
www.papercalculator.org

CONTENTS

for my mother

Joanne Cornbleet

ACKNOWLEDGMENTS

Thank you from my heart to the staff of Living Light Culinary Arts Institute, including Cherie Soria, Dan Ladermann, Kari Bernardi, Steve Claus, Patricia Hoskins, Elaina Love, Martine Lussier, Brenda O'Bryant, Inga Peterson, Matt Samuelson, Kristin Suratt, and Hilloah Tanner. My journey into this profession began with learning from and working with you. Special thanks to Cherie for our friendship and for years of creative work together. And to all the graduates of Living Light whom I've had the pleasure to teach.

I feel tremendous gratitude to the staff of the Book Publishing Company—including Bob and Cynthia Holzapfel, Thomas Hupp, Barb Bloomfield, Anna Pope, Warren and Barbara Jefferson, Kathleen Rosemary, Rick Diamond, and Jo Stepaniak—for your incredible support to me personally, and for your three-decade commitment to publishing vegetarian and raw-food books. Thank you to my publicist, Frank Martin, for working so hard this year to promote *Raw Food Made Easy*. And also to Larry Cook, for producing and directing the *Raw Food Made Easy* DVD.

My thanks to the marketing directors of Whole Foods Markets in Chicago, including Andrew Wickwire, Perri Kramer, Troy Authement, and Rick Crump, for promoting raw-food classes in Chicago. And also to Judith Friedman and the Natural Gourmet Institute of New York for your generosity to me personally and for including raw food in your curriculum.

I appreciate my friend Bill Veeder for brainstorming and editing sessions, and for being a good-natured guinea pig during recipe testing.

My heartfelt thanks to Keyvan Golestaneh, the practitioner of natural medicine and healer who introduced me to raw food. Your guidance and wisdom continue to bless my life.

I want to express my gratitude to my assistant Laura Williams—your help with classes, recipe testing, and organization made it possible for me to still have a life while working on so many projects. I wish you all the best in your future endeavors. Thank you also to Carol Rodgers for being a master recipe tester, to Bennett McClellan and Caroline Dowdy for your invaluable help and support with the photo shoot, and to my class assistants, including Connie Lambert, Ellie Welton, Linda Szarkowski, Bonnie Carter, and Nancy Gilbert.

Finally, my inexpressible gratitude to my Beloved Spiritual Master, Adi Da Samraj, for showing me faith in something greater in life.

INTRODUCTION

Exquisite desserts began appearing in the best raw-food restaurants and cafés several years ago. No longer did we have to settle for seventies-style, heavy-as-bricks date-almond balls. I began to wonder—how many of our favorite treats could feature unprocessed ingredients? And still taste amazing? For everyone? *Raw for Dessert* is my answer.

In this book you'll find recipes that are innovative, delicious, and easy. Innovative, because we need an alternative to the past. We can eliminate animal products (including milk, cream, butter, and eggs), processed foods (white flour, white sugar, corn syrup, trans fats, and chemicals), and even the age-old tradition of baking itself. No more rolling a piecrust into a ragged attempt at a circle; no more burning the cookies or failing to boil candy to the elusive soft-ball stage. Instead we can practice the art of substitution—to create traditional-tasting cakes, cookies, pies, creamy desserts, ice creams, and candies. Ground nuts replace flour; dried fruits and other natural sweeteners replace sugar; and avocados and coconut replace butter, cream, and eggs. When traditional tastes can be enhanced by small amounts of non-raw ingredients, however, I offer them as an option.

The results are consistently delicious. Fruit desserts rely on minimal ingredients to highlight their natural sweetness, shapes, and colors. These desserts are great for every day. Richer treats can also be free of gluten and dairy products and provide health-promoting vitamins, enzymes, and fiber—while tasting as good as or better than traditional versions. Imagine raw coconut cream pie, pineapple upside-down cake, cookies 'n' cream ice cream . . . and lots and lots of chocolate—desserts don't have to be damaging to be delicious.

They also don't need to be difficult to prepare. Easy was my goal with *Raw Food Made Easy for 1 or 2 People*, and it remains so in *Raw for Dessert*. We're all too busy in today's hectic world to toil away in the kitchen when wonderful, healthful recipes can be made for a reasonable amount of money, in a reasonable amount of time. A blender, a food processor, and a modest group of implements are all you need. Inevitably, a few recipes are a bit more challenging. So I encourage you to read Essential Information (pages 3–13) before you begin the adventure.

ere is a list of the ingredients and equipment you need to have, plus the techniques you need to know, to make the recipes in this book. I've defined what may be unfamiliar. All ingredients and equipment can be purchased online; for recommended brands and where to find them, visit my website, www.learnrawfood.com, and go to the "shop" tab.

ESSENTIAL INFORMATION

Ingredients

If you have these staples on hand, you'll need to purchase only fresh fruit and mint in order to make any dessert in this book. Keep spices and dried fruits in a cool, dark cabinet, away from direct heat and light, for one year. Store virgin coconut oil at room temperature for six months. Dates will keep at room temperature for two months, in the refrigerator for six months, or in the freezer for one year. Make sure that the nuts you purchase are raw, not roasted. Store them in sealed containers in the refrigerator for three months or in the freezer for one year.

agar flakes Agar is a vegetarian (but not raw) gelatin substitute made from various sea vegetables. It is flavorless and becomes gelatinous when dissolved in water, heated, and cooled.

agave syrup, raw (also called agave nectar) Agave syrup is a natural sweetener made from the juice of the agave plant. Choose light agave syrup for a mild sweetness, and dark for a deep, molasses-like flavor. Maple syrup may be substituted.

almond extract

almonds, whole and sliced

apricots, dried

blackberries, frozen organic

Brazil nuts

cacao nibs, raw Raw cacao nibs are lightly crushed cacao beans. Their taste is nicely bittersweet. If raw cacao nibs are unavailable, miniature vegan chocolate chips are a non-raw alternative.

carob powder Carob powder is a dark brown powder made from ground carob seeds and pods. It tastes similar to cocoa powder and has no caffeine. It may be purchased raw or roasted.

cashew butter, raw Raw cashew butter can be found at most natural food stores. To make your own, place 3 cups of unsoaked raw cashews or cashew pieces in a food processor fitted with the S blade and process until the cashews are ground to a smooth paste (this will take five to ten minutes). Stop occasionally to scrape down the sides of the work bowl with a rubber spatula. Stored in a sealed container in the refrigerator, cashew butter will keep for one month.

cashews, raw Most cashew nuts that are labeled "raw" are not; they've been heat-processed to remove the nut from the shell. Truly raw cashews are available online.

cayenne

cherries, dried

cherries, frozen organic

cardamom, ground

cinnamon, ground

cloves, ground

cocoa powder or raw cacao powder Cocoa powder is made from roasted cacao beans that have been processed to extract the butter, then dried and ground. Choose an organic brand. (Dutch-processed cocoa powders, such as Green and Black's, are my favorite because they have the deepest chocolate flavor.) Raw cacao powder can be purchased at some natural food stores or online.

coconut, unsweetened shredded dried

coconut oil, virgin (also called virgin coconut butter) Virgin coconut oil is unrefined and raw. It is solid at cool temperatures, which makes it an ideal replacement for butter in raw desserts. I recommend Jungle brand extra-virgin coconut oil. To use coconut oil in blended recipes, you must melt it first. To do this, fill a saucepan with several inches of water and bring to a boil. Turn off the heat, place the jar of coconut oil in the hot water, and let it sit for twenty minutes. Alternatively, warm the oil in a food dehydrator at 105 degrees F for twenty minutes. The coconut oil at the top of the jar will become liquid; without stirring, pour into a measuring cup the amount required by the recipe.

coconuts, young Young coconuts are harvested early—for their soft meat and sweet water. Thai young coconuts, as they are commonly called in the United States, are white, since they have already been husked. Each coconut provides approximately one-half cup of meat. See page 11 for instructions on how to open a young coconut. Whole young coconuts can be stored in the refrigerator for two weeks; the meat will keep for two months in the freezer.

cranberries, dried

currants

curry powder

dates, medjool

ginger, ground

honey, raw Raw honey has not been heat-processed. Vegans can substitute light agave syrup.

maple syrup Maple syrup isn't raw. Substitute dark agave syrup, if preferred.

nutmeg, ground

pecans

pine nuts

pistachios

pumpkin pie spice

raisins, dark and golden

raspberries, frozen organic

rose water Rose water is a fragrant liquid made by distilling rose petals. It is commonly used in Indian and Middle Eastern desserts.

salt, unrefined Sun-dried salt has its natural mineral content intact. I recommend Celtic Sea Salt or Himalayan Crystal Salt.

soy lecithin powder Soy lecithin, while not raw, makes desserts firmer and creamier. Use the powdered form, as the coarse granules do not break down completely when processed in a blender. I like Health Alliance brand non-GMO lecithin powder. (If you can't find powdered soy lecithin, grind the coarse granulated form in a coffee grinder.)

sugar, whole cane Whole cane sugar is unrefined and light brown in color. Rapadura and Sucanat are popular brands.

turmeric

vanilla beans To remove the seeds from a vanilla bean, lay the bean flat on a cutting board. Use a paring knife to split the bean lengthwise, then scrape out the seeds with the edge of the knife.

vanilla extract

walnuts

Equipment

Each recipe specifies the equipment and tools needed to make it. Here is a comprehensive list of all the implements called for in this book.

apple corer An apple corer is a tool with a medium-length shaft and a circular cutting ring at the end. The apple's core can be cut out with this tool while leaving the fruit intact. (Do not use the spoked-wheel type of corer that cuts the apple into wedges.)

baking cups, paper, 1¾ x 1-inch

baking pan, glass, 8-inch square

blender A blender is an electric appliance that purées and liquifies. There are several good, basic blenders; I like the KitchenAid KSB560 and the two-speed Oster Classic. For a powerful high-speed machine, you can't beat the Vita-Mix.

cake pans, 6-inch Though a standard cake pan is 8 to 9 inches in diameter, I recommend a smaller, 6-inch pan for raw cakes. This size allows you to create impressive-looking cakes while using less of each ingredient.

candy cups, foil, 1-inch

chef's knife A chef's knife is 7 to 10 inches long, with a broad blade and very sharp edge designed for slicing, chopping, dicing, and mincing.

citrus reamer or juicer Citrus reamers and juicers crush the flesh of halved citrus fruits, releasing their juice. Some manual models are handheld; others have a dish to catch the juice. Electric juicers are especially efficient when large quantities are needed.

cleaver A cleaver is the best knife for opening young coconuts.

cutting board

dehydrator A dehydrator is an electric appliance with low heat settings that can be used for making raw breads, crackers, and other dried foods. It can also warm up raw dishes.

file grater The tiny, razorlike edges of a file grater are ideal for removing the zest from citrus fruits. I recommend the Microplane brand. When zesting citrus fruits, do not include the bitter, white pith beneath the colored portion of the skin. If you don't have a file grater, use a zester.

food mill More effective than a fine-mesh strainer, a food mill creates a medium-bodied purée while straining out seeds and pulp.

food processor Fitted with an S blade, a food processor grinds and purées. It is indispensable for raw cakes, cookies, and pie and tart crusts.

ice-cream scoop An ice-cream scoop with a trigger handle releases the ice cream deftly.

ice cube trays, 3

ice-cream maker Modern ice-cream makers are inexpensive and easy to use (no hand-cranking, ice, or rock salt required). The canister, which holds a freezing agent, must be placed in the freezer for at least eight hours before using. I recommend the Cuisinart brand. You can purchase an extra bowl (or even two!) if you want to produce different flavors of ice cream in a row.

jars, quart-size

kitchen butane torch A kitchen butane torch is the best tool for creating a glasslike sugar surface without cooking the inside of the custard.

kitchen scissors

mandoline A mandoline is a hand-operated utensil with a variety of blades for slicing and julienning fruits and vegetables uniformly.

measuring cups and spoons

melon baller In addition to scooping out melon, a melon baller will remove the seeds and pith from apple and pear halves.

mesh bag Also called a sprout bag or nut-milk bag, a mesh bag is more effective than a strainer for extracting milk from blended nut mixtures.

miniature muffin pan A miniature muffin pan holds 24 tiny cupcakes, each about 1½ inches in diameter.

mixing bowls, small, medium, and large

parchment paper Parchment paper keeps ingredients from sticking to pans. To create a round of parchment, place a cake pan on top of a sheet of parchment paper. Trace the edge of the pan with a pencil. Remove the pan and cut out the outlined circle with kitchen scissors.

paring knife

peeler

pie pan, 9-inch

pie spatula A pie spatula has a wide, offset, triangular head.

saucepan, small

serrated knife, 5-inch A small, razor-sharp, maneuverable knife with a serrated edge is ideal for removing the peel from citrus fruits and for slicing soft fruits, such as nectarines and kiwifruit.

spatula, rubber

spatula, small, offset The slightly flexible blade of a small, offset spatula aids in spreading and smoothing frostings and fillings.

springform pan, 6- or 7-inch A springform pan, which has a clamp that releases the sides from the bottom, is essential for making cheesecakes. Choose a pan with a 6- or 7-inch diameter, rather than the standard 9-inch size, so you can use less of each ingredient while creating an impressive-looking cake.

squeeze bottles, 3

strainer, fine-mesh

tart pan, 9-inch A tart pan has straight sides with fluted edges. Choose one with a removable bottom, which allows you to release the outer ring while leaving the crust intact.

tartlet pans, 4½-inch

whisk

Serving Ware

It isn't essential to purchase all of these plates, bowls, and glasses (blackberry sorbet still tastes delicious in a bowl rather than a martini glass). But the serving ware listed below will give variety and elegance to your dessert presentations.

custard cups, glass or ceramic (or small coffee cups)

fluted dishes, shallow, 2- or 4-ounce Shallow, fluted dishes are best for serving Crème Brulée (page 101).

glasses, various sizes and shapes (wine, parfait, martini, and shot glasses) Glasses in various shapes and sizes are great for ice creams, sorbets, granitas, sundaes, and custards.

gratin dishes Gratin dishes are wide and shallow, making them perfect for fruit crumbles.

ice-cream dishes, glass, ceramic, or stainless steel

plates, white, various sizes and shapes (round, rectangular, and/or square)

ramekins, 6-ounce Ramekins, small ceramic dishes about 3 inches in diameter, are ideal for individual servings of crumbles and custards.

soup plates Deep, wide-rimmed soup plates look more elegant than bowls for fruit soup.

Techniques

Making raw desserts is basically as easy as pie. The few techniques that are intricate I'll explain here.

SOAKING NUTS

Many dessert recipes call for unsoaked nuts because a crumbly texture is preferred. To obtain the smooth texture necessary for nondairy milks, ice creams, and sauces, begin by soaking the nuts in a jar or bowl of cool water. Let the nuts soak for 8 to 12 hours, then drain and rinse them. They are now ready to be blended. Stored in a covered container in the refrigerator, soaked nuts will keep for 2 days.

OPENING YOUNG COCONUTS

This process may seem difficult at first, but you'll get the hang of it.

First, lay the coconut on its side on a cutting board. Using a cleaver, shave off the outer layer of the cone all around, until the brown inner shell is showing.

Now your goal is to cut into the cone deep enough so that you can pry off the top of the coconut. To accomplish this, strike the cone with the cleaver approximately 2 inches from the cone's point. The cleaver blade should lodge in the shell but should not cut the top off (or you'll spill the water inside). With one hand on the coconut and one on the embedded cleaver, lift up the coconut and cleaver simultaneously (keeping the side of the coconut parallel to the cutting board). Bang the coconut down on the board hard enough to produce a deep cut.

Then turn the coconut upright and set it on the cutting board. Pull off the top of the cone with your fingers. Pour the coconut water into a bowl or jar.

With a large spoon, scoop out the meat from the underside of the coconut's top. To get at the meat within the coconut itself, turn the spoon over and gently insert its edge between the shell and the meat. Proceed down into the coconut, scooping all around until the meat is extracted. (If brown bits of the inner shell adhere to the meat, scrape them off with a paring knife).

Knife Skills

While many desserts in this book require only a blender or a food processor, recipes with fruit involve some knife work. Here I'll review both general knife skills and the particular techniques required for certain fruits.

Begin by determining how the ingredient needs to be cut for the recipe. Sliced, diced, or minced? Slicing divides the fruit into relatively thin pieces, either lengthwise or crosswise. Dicing produces small cubes, about one-quarter inch. Mincing chops the fruit finely.

Learning basic knife techniques can both improve the appearance of your dishes and simplify kitchen work. For firm or large fruits, such as apples, pears, and pineapple, a 7- to 10-inch chef's knife is essential. For softer fruits, such as citrus, kiwifruit, and nectarines, a 5-inch serrated knife is easier.

To slice. When a chef's knife is required, place its tip on the cutting board beyond the far side of the fruit. (The middle portion of the blade will be doing the cutting.) Bring the handle gently down and push forward. Pull back and repeat. Use your free hand to hold the fruit, with your fingertips safely tucked under your knuckles. When using a serrated knife, move the blade back and forth in a sawing motion.

To dice. Use either a chef's or a serrated knife (depending on the fruit) to first cut the fruit into long strips. Then turn the strips sideways and slice them into 1/4-inch cubes.

To mince. Use the "fan technique" with ingredients such as fresh mint or dried fruit. Gather the ingredients in a pile on the cutting board. Place the tip of the chef's knife on the far side of the pile. Rest your free hand on top of the blade. Keeping the knife tip on the board, move the blade up and down quickly as you pivot the handle in a fan motion. Stop periodically to reassemble the pile of ingredients, and continue mincing until a finely chopped texture is achieved.

CUTTING FRUITS

Oranges and grapefruits. To peel and segment an orange or grapefruit, begin by cutting off each end of the fruit with a small, serrated knife. Then set the fruit on end on a cutting board. Following down the curve of the fruit, cut away the peel on all sides. Holding the peeled fruit over a mixing bowl to catch the juices, use the knife to cut each segment out from between the white membranes. Squeeze the core to extract additional juice.

Avocados. To peel and mash an avocado, place it lengthwise on a cutting board. Cut into the peel with a chef's knife until it touches the pit. Then rotate the avocado vertically 360 degrees, keeping the knife against the pit. Twist the avocado to separate the halves. Push the blade hard into the pit and twist to pull the pit out. Scoop the flesh from the peel with a spoon, then mash it.

Mangoes. To slice a mango, cut off one end and set the fruit flat on a cutting board. Remove the skin in strips with a paring knife or peeler. Using a chef's knife, shave off thin slices of the flesh on all sides until you reach the pit. If a recipe requires you to dice the mango, begin by slicing the fruit lengthwise into quarters with a chef's knife, cutting all around the pit. Scoop the flesh away from the peel with a spoon, discard the peel, and dice the flesh into 1/4-inch cubes.

Apples and pears. To thinly slice an apple or pear, cut off each end of the fruit and then peel it. Set the fruit on end on a cutting board and cut it in half lengthwise. Using a melon baller or a teaspoon, scoop out the core and seeds. Place each half lengthwise on the board, cut-side down, and thinly slice.

Peaches and nectarines. To halve a peach or nectarine, place the blade of a chef's knife in the natural groove of the fruit. Press down until you reach the pit. Rotate the fruit vertically all the way around, continuing to press down on the pit. Twist the fruit to separate the halves. Push the lower part of the blade hard into the pit and twist the knife to pull the pit out.

Kiwifruit. To peel kiwifruit, cut off the top and bottom ends, and then peel down the sides with a paring knife or peeler. For full moons, slice the fruit thinly crosswise; for half-moons, slice in half lengthwise, then slice each half thinly crosswise.

Pineapple. To peel a pineapple, first cut off the top and bottom ends with a chef's knife. Set the pineapple upright and cut off the peel in a downward motion. Continue until you have removed the entire outer skin. (Use a paring knife to shave any remaining brown bits off the fruit.) Slice the pineapple lengthwise into quarters, cutting around the core. Next, thinly slice, cube, or dice the pineapple pieces.

et's begin with creams, sauces, toppings, frostings, and crusts. You can eat them on their own (it's hard to resist Chocolate Ganache straight out of the blender!). And by combining them with each other and with other ingredients, you can create dozens of recipes. For example, Pastry Cream *(page 20)* is the custard filling in Summer Fruit Trifle *(page 43)*, Classic Fresh Fruit Tart *(page 92)*, and Banana Cream Pie *(page 89)*. If you change a few ingredients and serve the Pastry Cream in shallow, fluted dishes, you will have Vanilla Bean Crème Brulée *(page 101)*. Chocolate Ganache *(page 26)* can be a frosting for Chocolate Cupcakes *(page 73)*, a sauce for a hot fudge sundae, or a fondue with fruit. Even crusts, such as Graham Crust *(page 31)* and Chocolate Cookie Crust *(page 30)*, are versatile. You can use them as shells for pies and tarts *(see pages 85–98)* or as crumbles for Apple-Pear Crumble *(page 46)* and Cookies 'n' Cream Ice Cream *(page 62)*.

BASICS

Almond milk replaces dairy milk and cream in many raw ice creams *(see pages 49–70)*. Try a tall, cold glass with cookies *(see pages 80–81)*, Really! One Bowl Brownies *(page 83)*, or Chocolate Cupcakes *(page 73)*.

almond milk

YIELD: 2 CUPS

INGREDIENTS

2 cups filtered water

1 cup raw almonds, soaked for 8 to 12 hours (1½ cups after soaking), drained and rinsed

1 tablespoon light agave syrup (optional)

EQUIPMENT

measuring cups

blender

mesh bag (see page 8)

medium mixing bowl

Place the water, almonds, and optional agave syrup in a blender. Process on high speed until very smooth. Strain through a mesh bag into a medium mixing bowl. Transfer to a jar and store in the refrigerator. Almond Milk tastes best if chilled for at least 2 hours before serving.

Stored in a sealed jar in the refrigerator, Almond Milk will keep for 5 days. It will separate, however, so shake well before serving.

ahead of time

Soak the almonds for 8 to 12 hours. Drain and rinse. Soaked almonds can be stored in the refrigerator for 2 days.

BRAZIL NUT MILK: Replace the almonds with raw Brazil nuts. Use as the base for Brazil Nut–Vanilla Ice Cream *(page 57)*, Cookies 'n' Cream Ice Cream *(page 62)*, Nectarines 'n' Cream Ice Cream *(page 58)*, Pralines 'n' Cream Ice Cream *(page 62)*, and Strawberries 'n' Cream Ice Cream *(page 58)*.

PISTACHIO MILK: Replace the almonds with raw pistachios and you have the base for Pistachio Ice Cream *(page 63)*.

COFFEE ALMOND MILK: Replace the filtered water with freshly brewed regular or decaffeinated coffee. Use as the base for Coffee Ice Cream *(page 60)*.

Date paste sweetens and thickens many raw desserts. It is the main ingredient in the filling for Chocolate Pecan Pie *(page 95)*.

date paste

YIELD: 2½ CUPS

INGREDIENTS

32 pitted medjool dates

3 cups filtered water

EQUIPMENT

measuring cups

medium mixing bowl

food processor

rubber spatula

Place the dates in a medium mixing bowl, cover with the water, and let soak for 20 minutes. Soften the dates by massaging them in the soaking water with your hands for a minute. Drain the dates but reserve the soaking water.

Place the dates along with ½ cup of the soaking water in a food processor fitted with the S blade and process into a smooth paste. Stop occasionally to scrape down the sides of the work bowl with a rubber spatula.

Stored in a sealed container, Date Paste will keep for 2 weeks in the refrigerator or for 1 month in the freezer. Thaw for a few minutes before serving.

ahead of time

Soak the dates for 20 minutes.

This dairy-free topping replaces whipped cream—without sacrificing flavor or richness. Try it with Summer Berry Compote *(page 37)* or Apple-Pear Crumble *(page 46)*.

vanilla cashew cream

YIELD: 1 CUP

INGREDIENTS

1 cup cashews, soaked for 8 to 12 hours (1¼ cups after soaking), drained and rinsed

¼ cup plus 2 tablespoons water

¼ cup light agave syrup or maple syrup

1 vanilla bean, seeds only (see page 6), **or 2 teaspoons vanilla extract**

EQUIPMENT

measuring cups and spoons

paring knife

cutting board

blender

rubber spatula

Place the cashews, water, and agave syrup in a blender and process until very smooth. Stop occasionally to scrape down the sides of the blender jar with a rubber spatula. Add the vanilla bean seeds and process until well combined. Chill in the refrigerator for at least 1 hour before serving.

Stored in a sealed container in the refrigerator, Vanilla Cashew Cream will keep for 5 days.

ahead of time

Soak the cashews for 8 to 12 hours. Drain and rinse. Soaked cashews can be stored in the refrigerator for 2 days.

Why must a cream topping always be vanilla? Try Chocolate Cashew Cream with Spice Cake *(page 77)* or Chocolate Cream Pie *(page 93)*.

chocolate cashew cream

YIELD: 1½ CUPS

INGREDIENTS

1 cup cashews, soaked for 8 to 12 hours (1¼ cups after soaking), drained and rinsed

½ cup water

¼ cup light agave syrup

¼ cup Date Paste (page 17)

2 tablespoons cocoa powder or raw cacao powder (see page 5)

1 teaspoon vanilla extract

EQUIPMENT

measuring cups and spoons

blender

rubber spatula

Place all of the ingredients in a blender and process until very smooth. Stop occasionally to scrape down the sides of the blender jar with a rubber spatula.

Stored in a sealed container in the refrigerator, Chocolate Cashew Cream will keep for 5 days.

ahead of time

Soak the cashews for 8 to 12 hours. Drain and rinse. Soaked cashews can be stored in the refrigerator for 2 days.

Young coconut meat is the secret ingredient here. It provides the color and texture of dairy cream—without the dairy. Use raw Pastry Cream in Classic Fresh Fruit Tart *(page 92)*, Cherry Custard Tart with Sliced Almonds *(page 91)*, and Banana Cream Pie *(page 89)*. Thank you to Elaina Love for this recipe.

pastry cream

YIELD: 2 CUPS

INGREDIENTS

1½ cups young coconut meat (from 3 coconuts; see page 5)

⅓ cup light agave syrup

⅓ cup water

1 tablespoon freshly squeezed orange juice

1 teaspoon vanilla extract, or 1 vanilla bean, seeds only (see page 6)

⅛ teaspoon salt

⅛ teaspoon almond extract

Pinch turmeric

2 tablespoons virgin coconut oil, melted (see page 5)

1 tablespoon soy lecithin powder (see page 6; optional)

EQUIPMENT

measuring cups and spoons

cutting board

cleaver

large spoon

paring knife

citrus juicer or reamer

small saucepan

blender

rubber spatula

Place the coconut meat, agave syrup, water, orange juice, vanilla extract, salt, almond extract, and turmeric in a blender and process until very smooth. Stop occasionally to scrape down the sides of the blender jar with a rubber spatula. Add the coconut oil and optional soy lecithin powder and process until smooth.

Stored in a sealed container in the refrigerator, Pastry Cream will keep for 3 days.

Lemon curd is a thick, soft, creamy custard with a wonderful tart yet sweet flavor. Enjoy it plain, substitute it for Pastry Cream in Summer Fruit Trifle *(page 43)*, or fill a Lemon Tart with it *(page 86)*.

lemon curd

YIELD: 2½ CUPS

INGREDIENTS

1½ cups young coconut meat (from 3 coconuts; see page 5)

¾ cup freshly squeezed lemon juice

¾ cup light agave syrup

¼ teaspoon salt

⅛ teaspoon turmeric

2 tablespoons virgin coconut oil, melted (see page 5)

1 tablespoon soy lecithin powder (see page 6; optional)

EQUIPMENT

measuring cups and spoons

cutting board

cleaver

large spoon

citrus juicer or reamer

small saucepan

blender

rubber spatula

Place the coconut meat, lemon juice, agave syrup, salt, and turmeric in a blender and process until very smooth. Add the coconut oil and optional soy lecithin powder and process until smooth. Chill in the refrigerator for at least 2 hours before serving.

Stored in a sealed container in the refrigerator, Lemon Curd will keep for 3 days.

ORANGE CURD: Replace the lemon juice with freshly squeezed orange juice. Omit the turmeric.

This silky green cream is an avant-garde twist on traditional white whipped toppings. It tastes fantastic with Mango-Raspberry Crumble *(page 45)* and Pineapple Upside-Down Cake *(page 72)*.

avocado crème anglaise

YIELD: ¾ CUP

INGREDIENTS

½ cup mashed avocado
(1 avocado)

¼ cup light agave syrup

2 tablespoons water

1 vanilla bean,
seeds only (see page 6),
**or 2 teaspoons vanilla
extract**

EQUIPMENT

measuring cups

small mixing bowl

cutting board

chef's knife

fork or whisk

tablespoon

paring knife

food processor

rubber spatula

Place all of the ingredients in a food processor fitted with the S blade and process until smooth. Stop occasionally to scrape down the sides of the work bowl with a rubber spatula.

Stored in a sealed container in the refrigerator, Avocado Crème Anglaise will keep for 3 days.

The perfect smoothness of this seedless raspberry sauce is what makes it so elegant. Try it drizzled on ice creams, sorbets, and sundaes *(see pages 49–70)*, or on a dessert plate beneath Chocolate Cake with Fudge Frosting *(page 74)*.

R*raspberry coulis*

YIELD: 1 CUP

INGREDIENTS

2 (10-ounce) **packages frozen raspberries,** thawed in the packages

¼ **cup light agave syrup**

EQUIPMENT

measuring cups

food mill or fine-mesh strainer

medium mixing bowl

whisk

Set a food mill fitted with the medium-fine disk over a medium mixing bowl. Pour the berries and their juice into the food mill. Turn the handle to produce a purée. Discard the seeds. Alternatively, place a fine-mesh strainer over a bowl and pour the berries and juice through it. Then use a rubber spatula to press down the pulp that's caught in the strainer. Add the agave syrup to the purée and whisk until smooth.

Stored in a sealed container in the refrigerator, Raspberry Coulis will keep for 5 days.

ahead of time

Thaw the frozen raspberries in the refrigerator for 24 hours or at room temperature for 8 to 12 hours.

BLACKBERRY COULIS: Replace the raspberries with thawed frozen blackberries.

A thicker, more textured alternative to Raspberry Coulis *(page 23)*, this jam is also the filling for Raspberry Squares *(page 82)*.

R raspberry jam

YIELD: ¾ CUP

INGREDIENTS

1 (10-ounce) package frozen raspberries, thawed and drained (¾ cup)

3 tablespoons Date Paste (page 17)

EQUIPMENT

medium mixing bowl

strainer or colander

measuring cups and spoons

small mixing bowl

fork or whisk

Place the raspberries and Date Paste in a small mixing bowl and stir with a fork or whisk until the paste is well incorporated. Chill in the refrigerator for at least 2 hours before serving.

Stored in a sealed container in the refrigerator, Raspberry Jam will keep for 5 days.

ahead of time

Thaw the frozen raspberries in the refrigerator for 24 hours or at room temperature for 8 to 12 hours.

blackberry sundae, page 68, and banana split, page 66

pineapple upside-down cake, page 72, with caramel sauce, facing page

This sauce is super as the filling for Chocolate-Caramel Lava Cake *(page 76)* and Caramel Apple Stacks *(page 44)* or as the topping for Turtle Sundae *(page 70)*.

caramel sauce

YIELD: 1 CUP

INGREDIENTS

½ cup raw cashew butter (see page 4)

½ cup maple syrup or dark agave syrup

½ cup Date Paste (page 17)

2 teaspoons vanilla extract, or 1 vanilla bean, seeds only (see page 6)

⅛ teaspoon salt

EQUIPMENT

measuring cups and spoons

blender

rubber spatula

Place all of the ingredients in a blender and process until smooth. Stop occasionally to scrape down the sides of the blender jar with a rubber spatula.

Stored in a sealed container in the refrigerator, Caramel Sauce will keep for 2 weeks. Once refrigerated, the sauce will need to be warmed before serving in order to obtain the proper consistency (see note).

NOTE: To warm the freshly made or refrigerated sauce, place about 2 inches of water in a saucepan and bring to a boil. Turn off the heat. Place a small bowl of the Caramel Sauce in the hot water and let sit for 10 minutes. The sides of the bowl should be high enough so that the water from the saucepan cannot flow into the bowl. Alternatively, place the bowl in a food dehydrator at 105 degrees F for 10 minutes.

"Ganache," the French term for a smooth mixture of chocolate and cream, is the classic base for truffles and frosting. My version replaces the traditional butter, cream, and refined sugar with virgin coconut oil and agave syrup. Try this ganache as a hot fudge sauce with Brazil Nut–Vanilla Ice Cream *(page 57)*, as a frosting for Chocolate Cupcakes *(page 73)*, or as a fondue with strawberries, orange segments, and slices of mangoes, bananas, and pears.

chocolate ganache

YIELD: 1 CUP

INGREDIENTS

¾ cup dark agave syrup or maple syrup

¾ cup cocoa powder or raw cacao powder (see page 5)

⅓ cup virgin coconut oil, melted (see page 5)

⅛ teaspoon plus a pinch salt

EQUIPMENT

measuring cups and spoons

small saucepan

blender

rubber spatula

Place all of the ingredients in a blender and process until smooth. Stop occasionally to scrape down the sides of the blender jar with a rubber spatula.

Stored in a sealed container in the refrigerator, Chocolate Ganache will keep for 2 weeks. Once refrigerated, the ganache will need to be warmed before serving in order to obtain the proper consistency (see note).

NOTE: To warm the freshly made or refrigerated ganache, place about 2 inches of water in a saucepan and bring to a boil. Turn off the heat. Place a small bowl of the Chocolate Ganache in the hot water and let sit for 10 minutes. The sides of the bowl should be high enough so that the water from the saucepan cannot flow into the bowl. Alternatively, place the bowl in a food dehydrator at 105 degrees F for 10 minutes.

German Chocolate Cake *(page 75)* is just chocolate cake until you put this frosting on it.

coconut-pecan frosting

YIELD: 1½ CUPS

INGREDIENTS

1 cup Date Paste
(page 17)

½ cup unsweetened shredded dried coconut

¼ cup raw pecans
(unsoaked), finely chopped

EQUIPMENT

measuring cups

medium mixing bowl

cutting board

chef's knife

rubber spatula

Place the Date Paste and coconut in a medium mixing bowl and stir until well combined. Add the pecans and stir until evenly distributed.

Stored in a sealed container in the refrigerator, Coconut Pecan Frosting will keep for 5 days.

You don't need butter and brown sugar to achieve a New Orleans–style praline. Use it in Pralines 'n' Cream Ice Cream *(page 62)* or sprinkle it on a Turtle Sundae *(page 70)*.

praline

YIELD: ¾ CUP (6 SERVINGS)

1 cup raw almonds (unsoaked)

½ teaspoon ground cinnamon

⅛ teaspoon salt

⅛ teaspoon ground nutmeg

6 tablespoons maple syrup or dark agave syrup

measuring cups and spoons

food processor

rubber spatula

Place the almonds, cinnamon, salt, and nutmeg in a food processor fitted with the S blade and pulse until coarsely chopped. Don't overprocess. Add the maple syrup and pulse briefly to combine.

Stored in a sealed container in the refrigerator, Praline will keep for 2 weeks.

Almonds, which are lower in fat than other nuts, allow for a light crust that complements the rich filling of Chocolate Pecan Pie *(page 95).*

almond-pecan crust

YIELD: 2 CUPS (ENOUGH FOR ONE 9-INCH PIE OR TART)

INGREDIENTS

¾ cup raw almonds
(unsoaked)

⅛ teaspoon salt

½ cup raw pecans
(unsoaked)

8 pitted medjool dates

EQUIPMENT

**measuring cups
and spoons**

food processor

rubber spatula

Place the almonds and salt in a food processor fitted with the S blade and process until coarsely ground. Add the pecans and process until both the almonds and pecans are finely ground. Add the dates and process until the mixture begins to stick together. Don't overprocess.

Stored in a sealed container, Almond-Pecan Crust will keep for 1 month in the refrigerator or for 3 months in the freezer. The crust doesn't need to be thawed before using.

How To Form a Pie or Tart Crust

Pour the crust crumbs into the pie or tart pan. Use a light circular motion with your palm and fingers to distribute the crumbs uniformly along the bottom. Gently push some of the crumbs up the sides of the pan to the rim in order to create a ¼-inch-thick, loosely packed wall. Next, press the crust on the bottom of the pan down with your fingers and palm (be especially firm where the bottom of the pan joins the sides). To finish, press with your thumb to consolidate the crust wall along the pan's sides.

This crust will make you forget your favorite chocolate cookie. Try it as the shell for Coconut Cream Pie *(page 88)* or mixed into Cookies 'n' Cream Ice Cream *(page 62)*. Or just eat it straight!

chocolate cookie crust

YIELD: 2 CUPS (ENOUGH FOR ONE 9-INCH PIE OR TART)

INGREDIENTS

¾ cup raw almonds (unsoaked)

½ cup whole cane sugar (see page 6)

⅛ teaspoon salt

¾ cup cocoa powder or raw cacao powder (see page 5)

¼ cup virgin coconut oil, melted (see page 5)

EQUIPMENT

small saucepan

measuring cups and spoons

food processor

rubber spatula

Place the almonds, sugar, and salt in a food processor fitted with the S blade and process until finely ground. Add the cocoa powder and process to incorporate. Add the coconut oil and process until the mixture begins to stick together. Don't overprocess.

Stored in a sealed container, Chocolate Cookie Crust will keep for 1 month in the refrigerator or for 3 months in the freezer. The crust doesn't need to be thawed before using.

Whole cane sugar and raisins give this crust a deep graham flavor. Try it with Banana Cream Pie *(page 89)* or Pumpkin Pie *(page 96)*.

graham crust

YIELD: 2 CUPS (ENOUGH FOR ONE 9-INCH PIE OR TART)

INGREDIENTS

1 cup raw walnuts (unsoaked)

¼ cup unsweetened shredded dried coconut

¼ cup whole cane sugar (see page 6)

Pinch salt

¼ cup raisins

4 pitted medjool dates

EQUIPMENT

measuring cups and spoons

food processor

rubber spatula

Place the walnuts, coconut, sugar, and salt in a food processor fitted with the S blade. Process until finely ground. Add the raisins and dates and process until the mixture begins to stick together. Don't overprocess.

Stored in a sealed container, Graham Crust will keep for 1 month in the refrigerator or for 3 months in the freezer. The crust doesn't need to be thawed before using.

This crust is rich, buttery, and crumbly—perfect for Lemon Tart *(page 86)* and Classic Fresh Fruit Tart *(page 92).*

shortbread crust

YIELD: 2½ CUPS (ENOUGH FOR ONE 9-INCH PIE OR TART)

INGREDIENTS

1 cup unsweetened shredded dried coconut

1 cup raw walnuts (unsoaked)

¼ teaspoon salt

6 pitted medjool dates

EQUIPMENT

measuring cups and spoons

food processor

rubber spatula

Place the coconut, walnuts, and salt in a food processor fitted with the S blade. Process until finely ground. Add the dates and process until the mixture begins to stick together. Don't over-process.

Stored in a sealed container, Shortbread Crust will keep for 1 month in the refrigerator or for 3 months in the freezer. The crust doesn't need to be thawed before using.

*F*ruit is the quintessential raw dessert. And it is blessedly healthful—low in fat and high in fiber, vitamin C, and antioxidants. Every season provides its delicacies: berries, cherries, and nectarines in the summer; citrus, apples, pears, and dried fruits in the winter; tropical varieties year-round.

To preserve nature's pure, fresh taste, keep your fruit desserts simple. For example, arrange a variety of room-temperature fruits in a bowl or on a platter, perhaps adding fresh plant leaves for decoration, and serve this "still life" with a small plate and knife for each diner. Or cut up one fruit (or several) and add a little lemon juice and agave syrup to draw out the juice. For other simple desserts, try Strawberries in Orange Juice *(page 34)*, Macerated Citrus *(page 38)*, Mango Carpaccio *(page 36)*, and Summer Berry Compote *(page 37)*. Richer fresh fruit desserts make an impressive finale to any meal— just add crumble toppings and creamy fillings to create Banana-Caramel Crumble *(page 47)*, Caramel Apple Stacks *(page 44)*, or Summer Fruit Trifle *(page 43)*.

FRUIT DESSERTS

This dessert couldn't be simpler or more nutritious, yet it gives an elegant finish to a summer meal.

strawberries in orange juice

YIELD: 2 SERVINGS

INGREDIENTS

1 cup (8 ounces) **fresh strawberries,** thinly sliced

¼ cup freshly squeezed orange juice (½ medium orange)

EQUIPMENT

cutting board

small serrated knife or paring knife

citrus juicer or reamer

small mixing bowl

rubber spatula

Place the strawberries and orange juice in a small mixing bowl and toss gently to combine. Chill in the refrigerator for at least 15 minutes before serving.

Try this as a light first course or climactic dessert. Or, try it as a sauce with Strawberry Cheesecake (page 79).

strawberry soup

YIELD: 2 TO 3 SERVINGS

INGREDIENTS

2 cups (16 ounces) **fresh strawberries,** hulled

¼ cup plus 1 teaspoon light agave syrup

EQUIPMENT

cutting board

small serrated knife or paring knife

measuring cups and spoons

blender

rubber spatula

Thinly slice 3 of the strawberries. Place them in a small bowl with 1 teaspoon of the agave syrup and toss gently to combine. Set aside in the refrigerator.

Place the remaining strawberries and agave syrup in a blender and process until smooth. Chill in the refrigerator for at least 1 hour before serving. Serve in shallow soup plates or shot glasses, garnished with the reserved strawberry slices.

Stored in a sealed container in the refrigerator, Strawberry Soup will keep for 24 hours.

CREAM OF STRAWBERRY SOUP: Add ¼ cup of soaked raw cashews and 1 teaspoon of freshly squeezed lemon juice to the blender along with the strawberries and agave syrup. Process until very smooth. Garnish with the reserved strawberry slices or with Vanilla Cashew Cream *(page 18)* or Summer Berry Compote *(page 37)*.

"Carpaccio" is an Italian word that refers to ingredients that are sliced paper-thin and arranged attractively on a plate. Try dessert carpaccios made from any fruit you like, such as pineapples, melons, fresh figs, or pears.

mango carpaccio

YIELD: 2 SERVINGS

INGREDIENTS

2 ripe mangoes, thinly sliced

2 tablespoons light agave syrup

1 tablespoon freshly squeezed lemon juice

Pinch ground cinnamon

Fresh mint leaves (optional)

EQUIPMENT

measuring cups and spoons

citrus juicer or reamer

small mixing bowl

whisk

cutting board

paring knife

chef's knife

Arrange the mango slices on a plate. Place the agave syrup, lemon juice, and cinnamon in a small mixing bowl and whisk to combine. Drizzle over the mango slices. Chill in the refrigerator for at least 30 minutes before serving. Garnish with fresh mint leaves, if desired.

MANGO CARPACCIO WITH STRAWBERRIES AND KIWIFRUIT: Add $1/2$ cup (4 ounces) of thinly sliced strawberries and 1 kiwifruit, peeled and thinly sliced, to the plate of sliced mangoes.

This compote can provide a variety of pleasures—with Brazil–Nut Vanilla Ice Cream *(page 57)*, Cream of Strawberry Soup *(page 35)*, Raspberry Sorbet *(page 51)*, Strawberry Sorbet *(page 52)*, or Vanilla Cashew Cream *(page 18)*.

summer berry compote

YIELD: 4 SERVINGS

INGREDIENTS

1 cup (8 ounces) **fresh strawberries,** thinly sliced

½ cup (4 ounces) **fresh blueberries**

½ cup (4 ounces) **fresh raspberries**

½ cup (4 ounces) **fresh blackberries or additional raspberries**

2 tablespoons light agave syrup

1 tablespoon freshly squeezed lemon or lime juice

EQUIPMENT

measuring cups and spoons

cutting board

small serrated knife or paring knife

medium mixing bowl

citrus juicer or reamer

rubber spatula

Place all of the ingredients in a medium mixing bowl and toss gently to combine. Chill in the refrigerator for at least 15 minutes before serving.

Stored in a sealed container in the refrigerator, Summer Berry Compote will keep for 24 hours.

Refreshing and light, this is especially enjoyable in winter, when fewer fresh fruits are available.

*M*acerated citrus

YIELD: 2 TO 4 SERVINGS

INGREDIENTS

2 navel oranges, peeled and cut into segments (reserve juice)

1 grapefruit, peeled and cut into segments (reserve juice)

2 tablespoons light agave syrup

½ teaspoon orange zest (see page 8)

Fresh mint leaves (optional)

EQUIPMENT

cutting board

small serrated knife

measuring spoons

file grater or zester

medium mixing bowl

rubber spatula

Place the oranges, grapefruit, reserved juices, agave syrup, and orange zest in a medium mixing bowl and toss to combine. Chill in the refrigerator for at least 1 hour before serving. Garnish with fresh mint leaves, if desired.

Stored in a sealed container in the refrigerator, Macerated Citrus will keep for 24 hours.

MACERATED CITRUS WITH KIWIFRUIT: Add 2 kiwifruit, peeled and thinly sliced.

In Greek and Roman mythology, "ambrosia" means "food for the gods."

classic ambrosia

INGREDIENTS

2 oranges, peeled and cut into segments (reserve 2 tablespoons juice)

1 ripe banana, thinly sliced

⅓ cup unsweetened shredded dried coconut

1 tablespoon light agave syrup

EQUIPMENT

cutting board

small serrated knife

measuring cups and spoons

medium mixing bowl

strainer

rubber spatula

Place all of the ingredients in a mixing bowl and toss gently to combine. Chill in the refrigerator for at least 10 minutes before serving.

VARIATIONS: Add 1 or more of the following: ¼ cup of halved red or green seedless grapes; ¼ cup of cubed pineapple; 4 pitted medjool dates, coarsely chopped; and/or 2 tablespoons of chopped raw walnuts (unsoaked).

Delicious alone; divine as the filling for Tropical Ambrosia Tart *(page 90)*.

tropical ambrosia

INGREDIENTS

½ cup mashed avocado
(1 avocado)

¼ cup light agave syrup

2 tablespoons water

1 vanilla bean,
seeds only (see page 6),
or 2 teaspoons vanilla
extract

1 ripe banana, diced

1 ripe mango or ½ small
ripe papaya, diced

½ cup diced pineapple

EQUIPMENT

measuring cups

small mixing bowl

medium mixing bowl

cutting board

chef's knife

fork or whisk

tablespoon

paring knife

food processor

rubber spatula

Place the avocado, agave syrup, water, and vanilla bean seeds in a food processor fitted with the S blade and process until smooth. Stop occasionally to scrape down the sides of the work bowl with a rubber spatula. Transfer to a medium mixing bowl. Add the banana, mango, and pineapple and toss gently to combine. Chill in the refrigerator for at least 1 hour before serving.

Stored in a sealed container in the refrigerator, Tropical Ambrosia will keep for 24 hours.

This combination makes a fine finale to a fall or winter meal, served plain or with Brazil Nut–Vanilla Ice Cream *(page 57)*.

apple compote with golden raisins and pistachios

YIELD: 4 SERVINGS

INGREDIENTS

2 Gala or Granny Smith apples, or a combination, peeled and thinly sliced

2 tablespoons light agave syrup

1 tablespoon freshly squeezed lemon juice

¼ cup golden raisins

¼ cup raw pistachios (unsoaked), finely chopped

EQUIPMENT

cutting board

chef's knife

peeler

measuring cups and spoons

citrus juicer or reamer

medium mixing bowl

rubber spatula

Place the apples, agave syrup, and lemon juice in a medium mixing bowl and toss to combine. Massage the mixture gently with your hands to soften the apples (it's okay if some slices break). Add the raisins and pistachios and mix. Chill in the refrigerator for at least 1 hour before serving.

Stored in a sealed container in the refrigerator, Apple Compote will keep for 2 days.

NOTE: If you prefer the compote warm, heat it gently on the stove for a few minutes, taking care not to overheat it.

The vanilla bean gives this compote a magical fragrance. Serve it plain, as the filling for Mince Pie *(page 98)*, or as a topping for Brazil Nut–Vanilla Ice Cream *(page 57)* or Spice Cake *(page 77)*.

winter fruit compote

YIELD: 6 TO 8 SERVINGS

INGREDIENTS

1 cup freshly squeezed orange juice

⅔ cup golden raisins

⅔ cup dried apricots, minced

½ cup currants

½ cup dried cherries, minced

⅓ cup light agave syrup

2 vanilla beans, seeds removed (see page 6)

EQUIPMENT

measuring cups and spoons

cutting board

chef's knife

paring knife

citrus juicer or reamer

medium mixing bowl

rubber spatula

Place all of the ingredients, including the scraped vanilla bean pods and seeds, in a medium mixing bowl and soak at room temperature for 8 to 12 hours. Discard the vanilla bean pods. Serve at room temperature.

Stored in a sealed container in the refrigerator, Winter Fruit Compote will keep for 5 days.

NOTE: If you prefer the compote warm, heat it gently on the stove for a few minutes, taking care not to overheat it.

A British dessert made from layered custard, fruit, and cake, trifle is a stunning study in colors, textures, and flavors. Serve this raw version in a large glass bowl, family-style, or in individual glasses or custard cups. Make sure the cups are glass so you can show off all those layers.

summer fruit trifle

See photo between pages 56 and 57.

YIELD: 4 SERVINGS

INGREDIENTS

1 cup Shortbread Crust (page 32)

2 cups Pastry Cream (page 20), **Lemon Curd** (page 21), **or Orange Curd** (page 21)

2 cups Summer Berry Compote (page 37)

EQUIPMENT

measuring cups

medium glass serving bowl, or 4 wine glasses or custard cups

rubber spatula or large spoon

For family-style presentation, spread a layer of ½ cup of the Shortbread Crust in the bottom of a medium glass serving bowl. Add a layer of 1 cup of the Pastry Cream followed by a layer of 1 cup of the Summer Berry Compote, pressing down lightly on each layer with a rubber spatula or spoon. Repeat the layers of crust, cream, and fruit.

For individual servings, layer the ingredients in 4 wine glasses or custard cups. Use 2 tablespoons of the crust, ¼ cup of the cream, and ¼ cup of the fruit for each layer.

Chill in the refrigerator for at least 1 hour before serving. Covered with plastic wrap and stored in the refrigerator, Summer Fruit Trifle will keep for 24 hours.

With its gooey mask of caramel, this dessert is an elegant variation of a candy apple. Try it for Halloween or as the finale to a special fall meal.

caramel apple stacks

YIELD: 2 SERVINGS

INGREDIENTS

1 Gala apple

¼ cup Caramel Sauce (page 25), warmed

¼ cup Vanilla Cashew Cream (page 18)

EQUIPMENT

small saucepan

cutting board

apple corer

chef's knife or mandoline (see page 8)

measuring cups

2 rubber spatulas or spoons

Core the apple. With a chef's knife or mandoline, thinly slice the apple crosswise. For each stack, lay one apple slice on a plate and cover with some of the Caramel Sauce. Continue to layer 3 or 4 more slices, alternating with the sauce. Top with the Vanilla Cashew Cream and serve immediately.

This homey dessert makes a comforting end to a summer meal. Serve it on a pool of Vanilla Cashew Cream *(page 18)* or Avocado Crème Anglaise *(page 22)*.

mango-raspberry crumble

YIELD: 4 SERVINGS

INGREDIENTS

2 ripe mangoes, cubed

1 cup fresh raspberries

4 teaspoons light agave syrup

2 teaspoons freshly squeezed lemon juice

½ cup Shortbread Crust (page 32)

EQUIPMENT

cutting board

peeler

chef's knife

measuring cups and spoons

citrus juicer or reamer

medium mixing bowl

fork

4 (6-ounce) **ramekins or gratin dishes**

Place the mangoes, raspberries, agave syrup, and lemon juice in a medium mixing bowl and toss with a fork, lightly mashing the raspberries. Transfer the fruit mixture to 4 (6-ounce) ramekins or gratin dishes and top each serving with 2 tablespoons of the Shortbread Crust. Serve at room temperature.

Covered with plastic wrap and stored in the refrigerator, Mango-Raspberry Crumble will keep for 3 days.

NECTARINE-RASPBERRY CRUMBLE: Replace the mangoes with 2 ripe nectarines, thinly sliced.

Apple and pear make a succulent combination that is sweeter and softer than apples alone. Serve Apple-Pear Crumble on a pool of Vanilla Cashew Cream *(page 18)* or with Brazil Nut–Vanilla Ice Cream *(page 57)* or Pralines 'n' Cream Ice Cream *(page 62)*.

apple-pear crumble

YIELD: 4 SERVINGS

INGREDIENTS

1 apple, peeled, halved, and thinly sliced

1 pear, peeled, halved, and thinly sliced

1 teaspoon freshly squeezed lemon juice

¼ cup raisins or dried cranberries (optional)

1 apple, peeled and chopped

¼ cup Date Paste (page 17)

2 tablespoons freshly squeezed orange juice

Pinch ground cinnamon

Pinch ground nutmeg

1 cup Graham Crust (page 31)

EQUIPMENT

cutting board

peeler

chef's knife

measuring cups and spoons

citrus juicer or reamer

medium mixing bowl

rubber spatula

4 (6-ounce) **ramekins or gratin dishes**

Place the sliced apple, pear, and lemon juice in a medium mixing bowl and toss to combine. Add the optional raisins and toss again. Place the chopped apple, Date Paste, orange juice, cinnamon, and nutmeg in a food processor fitted with the S blade and process until smooth. Stop and scrape down the sides of the work bowl with a rubber spatula as needed. Add to the apple and pear slices and mix well with your hands to soften (it's okay if some slices break).

Place 2 tablespoons of the Graham Crust into each of 4 (6-ounce) ramekins or gratin dishes and press down. Add ½ cup of the fruit mixture to each ramekin. Top with 2 additional tablespoons of the crust, pressing it gently into the fruit. Serve at room temperature.

Covered with plastic wrap and stored in the refrigerator, Apple-Pear Crumble will keep for 3 days.

NOTE: If you prefer the crumble warm, preheat an oven to 200 degrees F. Turn off the oven, insert the ramekins, and warm them for 15 minutes. Alternatively, heat them in a food dehydrator at 105 degrees F for 30 minutes.

Delectable and rich. Try this as a winter dessert, a tea-time snack, or even a breakfast indulgence. Serve it plain or with Coconut Ice Cream *(page 65)*.

B banana-caramel crumble

YIELD: 4 SERVINGS

INGREDIENTS

1½ cups Shortbread Crust (page 32)

4 ripe bananas, sliced into large chunks

¼ cup Caramel Sauce (page 25)

EQUIPMENT

cutting board

chef's knife

medium mixing bowl

fork

measuring cups and spoons

4 (6-ounce) **ramekins or gratin dishes**

Place 1 cup of the Shortbread Crust and all of the bananas in a medium mixing bowl. Mash with a fork. Spoon the mixture equally into 4 (6-ounce) ramekins or gratin dishes. Top each serving with 1 tablespoon of the Caramel Sauce. Add 2 table-spoons of the remaining crust, pressing it lightly into the sauce with the fork. Serve immediately.

NOTE: If you prefer the crumble warm, preheat an oven to 200 degrees F. Turn off the oven, insert the ramekins, and warm them for 15 minutes. Alternatively, heat them in a food dehydrator at 105 degrees F for 30 minutes.

Made exclusively from fruit and agave syrup, sorbet is a naturally fat-free way to highlight the taste of fresh fruit. Also try granita, which has a pleasantly crunchy texture, like a snow cone.

If you want a richer frozen dessert, try my raw, dairy-free ice cream. With the exception of Banana–Chocolate Chip Ice Cream *(page 64)*, which derives its creaminess from bananas alone, my raw ice creams are made from nuts and/or young coconut meat instead of cow's milk and cream. Raw ice creams can be varied endlessly: Brazil Nut–Vanilla Ice Cream *(page 57)*, for example, becomes Chocolate Ice Cream *(page 59)*, Cookies 'n' Cream Ice Cream *(page 62)*, or Make a Mint Ice Cream *(page 61)* when you change a few ingredients.

Raw sundaes take a bit more planning, because they include several ice creams and/or sauces. But you can save time by making some of the components in advance. Additional equipment is needed for ice creams and sorbets. Modern ice-cream makers are inexpensive and easy to use (no hand-cranking, ice, or rock salt required). You can purchase an extra bowl (or even two!) if you want to produce different flavors of ice cream in a row *(see page 8)*. If you don't have an ice-cream maker, all you need is a food processor to make Grapefruit Granita *(page 56)*, Lemon Granita *(page 56)*, and Banana–Chocolate Chip Ice Cream *(page 64)*.

A food mill *(see page 8)* purées fruit and strains out the seeds, skins, and pulp to make the smoothest sorbets. If you don't have a food mill, a fine-mesh strainer will work.

SORBETS, ICE CREAMS, AND SUNDAES

Made with chocolate, water, and whole cane sugar only, this sorbet delivers undiluted chocolate intensity. Plus, it's fat free.

bitter chocolate sorbet

YIELD: 1½ CUPS (3 TO 4 SERVINGS)

INGREDIENTS

1 cup filtered water

½ cup whole cane sugar
(see page 6)

**⅓ cup cocoa powder
or raw cacao powder**
(see page 5)

Fresh raspberries
(optional)

EQUIPMENT

**measuring cups
and spoons**

blender

rubber spatula

jar

ice-cream maker

Place the water, sugar, and cocoa in a blender and process until very smooth. Transfer to a jar and chill in the refrigerator for at least 2 hours or up to 2 days. Put the mixture in an ice-cream maker and freeze according to the manufacturer's directions. Serve with fresh raspberries, if desired.

Bitter Chocolate Sorbet tastes best if eaten immediately, but it will keep for 5 days stored in a sealed container in the freezer. Thaw for a few minutes before serving.

B

blackberry sorbet

With its deep burgundy color, Blackberry Sorbet looks beautiful in a bowl by itself. For Blackberry Sundae *(page 68)*, use a tall parfait glass, alternating the sorbet with scoops of Brazil Nut–Vanilla Ice Cream *(page 57)* and topping the sundae with Blackberry Coulis *(page 23)* and fresh blackberries.

YIELD: 2 CUPS (4 SERVINGS)

INGREDIENTS

2 (10-ounce) **packages frozen blackberries,** thawed in the packages

¼ cup light agave syrup

Fresh blackberries (optional)

EQUIPMENT

measuring cups

food mill or fine-mesh strainer

medium mixing bowl

whisk

rubber spatula

jar

ice-cream maker

Set a food mill fitted with the medium-fine disk over a medium mixing bowl. Pour the berries and their juice into the food mill. Turn the handle to produce a purée. Discard the seeds. Alternatively, place a fine-mesh strainer over a bowl and pour the berries and juice through it. Then use a rubber spatula to press down the pulp that's caught in the strainer.

Add the agave syrup to the blackberry purée and whisk to combine. Transfer to a jar and chill in the refrigerator for at least 2 hours or up to 2 days. Put the blackberry mixture in an ice-cream maker and freeze according to the manufacturer's directions. Serve with fresh blackberries, if desired.

Blackberry Sorbet tastes best if eaten immediately, but it will keep for 5 days stored in a sealed container in the freezer. Thaw for a few minutes before serving.

ahead of time

Thaw the frozen blackberries in the refrigerator for 24 hours or at room temperature for 8 to 12 hours.

RASPBERRY SORBET: Replace the blackberries with thawed frozen raspberries.

Yes, there is strawberry heaven.

strawberry sorbet

YIELD: 2 CUPS (4 SERVINGS)

INGREDIENTS

2 cups (16 ounces)
fresh strawberries, hulled

¼ cup light agave syrup

Sliced fresh strawberries (optional)

EQUIPMENT

cutting board

paring knife

measuring cups

blender

rubber spatula

jar

ice-cream maker

Place the hulled strawberries and agave syrup in a blender and process until smooth. Transfer to a jar and chill in the refrigerator for at least 2 hours or up to 2 days. Put the strawberry mixture in an ice-cream maker and freeze according to the manufacturer's directions. Garnish with sliced fresh strawberries, if desired.

Strawberry Sorbet tastes best if eaten immediately, but it will keep for 5 days stored in a sealed container in the freezer. Thaw for a few minutes before serving.

Outrageously purple and packed with flavor, this sorbet is scrumptious alone or as a counterpoint to Red, White, and Blue Cheesecake *(page 78)*.

concord grape sorbet

YIELD: 2 CUPS (4 SERVINGS)

INGREDIENTS

4 cups Concord grapes (see note), stemmed and washed

¼ cup light agave syrup

EQUIPMENT

measuring cups

blender

rubber spatula

food mill or fine-mesh strainer

medium mixing bowl

whisk

rubber spatula

jar

ice-cream maker

Place the grapes in a blender and process for a few seconds. Don't overprocess. Set a food mill fitted with the medium-fine disk over a medium mixing bowl. Pour the grape mixture into the food mill. Turn the handle to produce a purée. Discard the skins and seeds. Alternatively, place a fine-mesh strainer over a bowl and pour the grape mixture through it. Then use a rubber spatula to press down the pulp that's caught in the strainer.

Add the agave syrup to the grape purée and whisk to combine. Transfer to a jar and chill in the refrigerator for at least 2 hours or up to 2 days. Put the grape mixture in an ice-cream maker and freeze according to the manufacturer's directions.

Concord Grape Sorbet tastes best if eaten immediately, but it will keep for 5 days stored in a sealed container in the freezer. Thaw for a few minutes before serving.

NOTE: Concord grapes are dark blue or purple and highly aromatic. They have a short growing season in the fall. If Concord grapes are not available, substitute red seedless grapes.

The lusciousness of fresh pineapple is captured in the soft color and sweet taste of this sorbet. Serve plain or on top of a pool of kheer *(page 100)*.

pineapple sorbet

YIELD: **2 CUPS** (4 SERVINGS)

INGREDIENTS

1 pineapple, cut into 1-inch cubes (3 cups)

½ cup light agave syrup

1 tablespoon freshly squeezed lemon juice

EQUIPMENT

measuring cups and spoons

food mill or fine-mesh strainer

medium mixing bowl

rubber spatula

jar

ice-cream maker

Place the pineapple in a blender and process until smooth. Set a food mill fitted with the medium-fine disk over a medium mixing bowl. Pour the pineapple mixture into the food mill. Turn the handle to produce a purée. Discard any remaining pulp. Alternatively, place a fine-mesh strainer over a bowl and pour the pineapple mixture through it. Then use a rubber spatula to press down the pulp that's caught in the strainer.

Add the agave syrup and lemon juice to the pineapple purée and whisk to combine. Transfer to a jar and chill in the refrigerator for at least 2 hours or up to 2 days. Put the pineapple mixture in an ice-cream maker and freeze according to the manufacturer's directions.

Pineapple Sorbet tastes best if eaten immediately, but it will keep for 5 days stored in a sealed container in the freezer. Thaw for a few minutes before serving.

Serve plain or topped with Macerated Citrus *(page 38)* or Classic Ambrosia *(page 39)* and a fresh mint sprig.

orange sorbet

See photo facing page 56. **YIELD: 3 CUPS** (4 TO 6 SERVINGS)

INGREDIENTS

2½ cups freshly squeezed orange juice

⅓ cup light agave syrup

EQUIPMENT

cutting board

small serrated knife

citrus juicer or reamer

measuring cups

medium mixing bowl

whisk

rubber spatula

jar

ice-cream maker

Place the orange juice and agave syrup in a medium mixing bowl and whisk to combine. Transfer to a jar and chill in the refrigerator for at least 2 hours or up to 2 days. Place the orange juice mixture in an ice-cream maker and freeze according to the manufacturer's directions.

Orange Sorbet tastes best if eaten immediately, but it will keep for 5 days stored in a sealed container in the freezer. Thaw for a few minutes before serving.

TANGERINE SORBET: Replace the orange juice with freshly squeezed tangerine juice.

LEMON SORBET: Replace the orange juice with ¾ cup of freshly squeezed lemon juice, add 1½ cups of water, increase the agave syrup to ¾ cup, and add a pinch of salt. Proceed as directed for Orange Sorbet.

This shimmering pink crushed ice is a grown-up slushy. It's a great palette cleanser between courses or at the end of a meal.

grapefruit granita

See photo on the facing page.　　　　**YIELD: 2½ CUPS** (4 SERVINGS)

INGREDIENTS

1½ cups freshly squeezed ruby red grapefruit juice
(3 grapefruits)

½ cup filtered water

⅓ cup light agave syrup

4 fresh mint sprigs
(optional)

EQUIPMENT

cutting board

small serrated knife

citrus juicer or reamer

measuring cups

medium mixing bowl

whisk

rubber spatula

3 standard ice cube trays

food processor

Place the grapefruit juice, water, and agave syrup in a medium mixing bowl and whisk to combine. Pour into 3 standard ice cube trays and set in the freezer for 4 to 12 hours.

Place the cubes from one tray in a food processor fitted with the S blade. Pulse about 12 times, in bursts of 2 to 3 seconds, until slushy. Remove and repeat with the remaining trays' cubes. Serve immediately, garnishing each serving with a sprig of mint, if desired.

ahead of time

Juice the grapefruits. Add the water and agave syrup and whisk to combine. Pour into 4 ice cube trays and set in the freezer for 4 to 12 hours. For longer storage, the frozen cubes can be transferred to zipper-lock plastic bags and stored in the freezer for 1 week.

LEMON GRANITA: Replace the grapefruit juice with ¾ cup of freshly squeezed lemon juice, increase the water to 1½ cups, increase the agave syrup to ¾ cup, and add a pinch of salt. Proceed as directed for Grapefruit Granita. Yield: 3 cups (6 servings).

foreground: grapefruit granita, page 56, background: orange sorbet, page 55

summer fruit trifle, page 43

classic fresh fruit tart, page 92

pumpkin pie, page 96, with vanilla cashew cream, page 18

What makes this vanilla ice cream special is the luxuriant richness of Brazil nuts. Serve it topped with Apple Compote with Pistachios and Golden Raisins *(page 41)*, Raspberry Coulis *(page 23)*, Summer Berry Compote *(page 37)*, Winter Fruit Compote *(page 42)*, or warmed Chocolate Ganache *(page 26)* for a hot fudge sundae.

brazil nut–vanilla ice cream

YIELD: 3 CUPS (4 TO 6 SERVINGS)

INGREDIENTS

2 cups Brazil Nut Milk (page 16), unsweetened

½ cup raw cashews, soaked for 8 to 12 hours (⅔ cup after soaking), drained and rinsed

½ cup light agave syrup

2 teaspoons vanilla extract

2 vanilla beans, seeds only (see page 6)

⅛ teaspoon salt

EQUIPMENT

measuring cups and spoons

cutting board

paring knife

blender

rubber spatula

jar

ice-cream maker

Pour ½ cup of the Brazil Nut Milk and all of the cashews in a blender and process until very smooth. Add the remaining 1½ cups Brazil Nut Milk and all of the agave syrup, vanilla extract, vanilla bean seeds, and salt and process until blended. Transfer to a jar and chill in the refrigerator for at least 2 hours or up to 2 days. Put the mixture in an ice-cream maker and freeze according to the manufacturer's directions.

Brazil Nut–Vanilla Ice Cream tastes best if eaten immediately, but it will keep for 5 days stored in a sealed container in the freezer. Thaw for a few minutes before serving.

ahead of time

Soak the Brazil nuts and cashews for 8 to 12 hours. Drain and rinse. The soaked nuts can be stored in the refrigerator for 2 days.

The magic of strawberries is often lost in the homogeneous pink of commercial ice cream brands. My raw alternative features bits of whole strawberries suspended in luxuriant cream.

strawberries 'n' cream ice cream

YIELD: 3 CUPS (4 TO 6 SERVINGS)

INGREDIENTS

1½ cups finely chopped strawberries

½ cup plus 1 tablespoon light agave syrup

2 cups Brazil Nut Milk (page 16), unsweetened

½ cup raw cashews, soaked for 8 to 12 hours (⅔ cup after soaking), drained and rinsed

1 teaspoon vanilla extract

⅛ teaspoon salt

EQUIPMENT

measuring cups and spoons

cutting board

paring knife

blender

rubber spatula

jar

ice-cream maker

Place the strawberries and 1 tablespoon of the agave syrup in a medium mixing bowl. Toss and set aside.

Pour ½ cup of the Brazil Nut Milk and all of the cashews in a blender and process until very smooth. Add the remaining 1½ cups Brazil Nut Milk, the remaining ½ cup agave syrup, and all of the vanilla extract and salt and process until blended. Transfer to a jar, add the strawberry mixture, and stir to combine.

Chill in the refrigerator for at least 2 hours or up to 2 days. Put the mixture in an ice-cream maker and freeze according to the manufacturer's directions.

Strawberries 'n' Cream Ice Cream tastes best if eaten immediately, but it will keep for 5 days stored in a sealed container in the freezer. Thaw for a few minutes before serving.

ahead of time

Soak the Brazil nuts and cashews for 8 to 12 hours. Drain and rinse. The soaked nuts can be stored in the refrigerator for 2 days.

NECTARINES 'N' CREAM ICE CREAM: Replace the strawberries with an equal amount of finely chopped ripe nectarines.

Bring a big bowl.

chocolate ice cream

YIELD: 3 CUPS (4 TO 6 SERVINGS)

INGREDIENTS

2 cups Almond Milk
(page 16), unsweetened

½ cup raw cashews,
soaked for 8 to 12 hours
(⅔ cup after soaking),
drained and rinsed

**½ cup cocoa powder
or raw cacao powder**
(see page 5)

½ cup light agave syrup

**2 teaspoons vanilla
extract**

⅛ teaspoon salt

EQUIPMENT

**measuring cups
and spoons**

cutting board

paring knife

blender

rubber spatula

jar

ice-cream maker

Pour ½ cup of the Almond Milk and all of the cashews in a blender and process until very smooth. Add the remaining 1½ cups Almond Milk and all of the cocoa, agave syrup, vanilla extract, and salt and process until blended. Transfer to a jar and chill in the refrigerator for at least 2 hours or up to 2 days. Put the mixture in an ice-cream maker and freeze according to the manufacturer's directions.

Chocolate Ice Cream tastes best if eaten immediately, but it will keep for 5 days stored in a sealed container in the freezer. Thaw for a few minutes before serving.

ahead of time

Soak the almonds and cashews for 8 to 12 hours. Drain and rinse. The soaked nuts can be stored in the refrigerator for 2 days.

My favorite.

coffee ice cream

INGREDIENTS

2 cups Coffee Almond Milk (page 16)

½ cup raw cashews, soaked for 8 to 12 hours (⅔ cup after soaking), drained and rinsed

½ cup light agave syrup

2 teaspoons vanilla extract

⅛ teaspoon salt

EQUIPMENT

measuring cups and spoons

blender

rubber spatula

jar

ice-cream maker

Pour 1 cup of the Coffee Almond Milk and all of the cashews in a blender and process until very smooth. Add the remaining 1 cup Coffee Almond Milk and all of the agave syrup, vanilla extract, and salt and process until blended. Transfer to a jar and chill in the refrigerator for at least 2 hours or up to 2 days. Put the mixture in an ice-cream maker and freeze according to the manufacturer's directions.

Coffee Ice Cream tastes best if eaten immediately, but it will keep for 5 days stored in a sealed container in the freezer. Thaw for a few minutes before serving.

ahead of time

Soak the almonds and the cashews for 8 to 12 hours. Drain and rinse. The soaked nuts can be stored in the refrigerator for 2 days.

This real mint ice cream tastes fresh and herbaceous—honestly different from the artificially flavored versions in most grocery stores and ice-cream parlors.

M make a mint ice cream

YIELD: **3 CUPS** (4 TO 6 SERVINGS)

INGREDIENTS

2 cups Almond Milk (page 16), unsweetened

½ cup raw cashews, soaked for 8 to 12 hours (⅔ cup after soaking), drained and rinsed

1 cup fresh mint leaves, packed

½ cup light agave syrup

1 teaspoon vanilla extract

⅛ teaspoon salt

EQUIPMENT

measuring cups and spoons

blender

rubber spatula

jar

ice-cream maker

Pour ½ cup of the Almond Milk and all of the cashews in a blender and process until very smooth. Add the mint leaves and process until smooth. Add the remaining 1½ cups Almond Milk and all of the agave syrup, vanilla extract, and salt and process until blended. Transfer to a jar and chill in the refrigerator for at least 2 hours or up to 2 days. Put the mixture in an ice-cream maker and freeze according to the manufacturer's directions.

Make a Mint Ice Cream tastes best if eaten immediately, but it will keep for 5 days stored in a sealed container in the freezer. Thaw for a few minutes before serving.

ahead of time

Soak the almonds and the cashews for 8 to 12 hours. Drain and rinse. The soaked nuts can be stored in the refrigerator for 2 days.

MINT CHIP ICE CREAM: Decrease the mint to ¾ cup, packed. Place ⅓ cup of cacao nibs (see page 4) in a food processor and pulse-chop until coarsely ground. Don't overprocess. Add the ground nibs to the ice-cream maker 30 seconds before you turn the machine off.

Why have cookies 'n' milk when you can have cookies 'n' cream?

cookies 'n' cream ice cream

YIELD: 3 CUPS (4 TO 6 SERVINGS)

INGREDIENTS

2 cups Brazil Nut Milk (page 16), unsweetened

½ cup raw cashews, soaked for 8 to 12 hours (⅔ cup after soaking), drained and rinsed

½ cup light agave syrup

2 teaspoons vanilla extract

⅛ teaspoon salt

½ cup Chocolate Cookie Crust (page 30)

EQUIPMENT

measuring cups and spoons

blender

rubber spatula

jar

ice-cream maker

Pour ½ cup of the Brazil Nut Milk and all of the cashews in a blender and process until very smooth. Add the remaining 1½ cups Brazil Nut Milk and all of the agave syrup, vanilla extract, and salt and process until blended. Transfer to a jar and chill in the refrigerator for at least 2 hours or up to 2 days. Put the mixture in an ice-cream maker and freeze according to the manufacturer's directions. Crumble the Chocolate Cookie Crust into the ice-cream maker 30 seconds before you turn the machine off.

Cookies 'n' Cream Ice Cream tastes best if served immediately, but it will keep for 5 days stored in a sealed container in the freezer. Thaw for a few minutes before serving.

ahead of time

Soak the Brazil nuts and cashews for 8 to 12 hours. Drain and rinse. The soaked nuts can be stored in the refrigerator for 2 days.

PRALINES 'N' CREAM ICE CREAM: Replace the Chocolate Cookie Crust with ½ cup of Praline (page 28).

pistachio ice cream

This lovely pale green ice cream treats you to the unmistakable flavor and crunch of pistachios.

YIELD: 3 CUPS (4 TO 6 SERVINGS)

INGREDIENTS

2 cups Pistachio Milk (page 16), unsweetened

½ cup raw cashews, soaked for 8 to 12 hours (⅔ cup after soaking), drained and rinsed

½ cup light agave syrup

¼ teaspoon almond extract

⅛ teaspoon salt

¼ cup raw pistachios, soaked for 8 to 12 hours (⅓ cup after soaking), drained, rinsed, and finely chopped

EQUIPMENT

measuring cups and spoons

cutting board

paring knife

blender

rubber spatula

jar

ice-cream maker

Pour ½ cup of the Pistachio Milk and all of the cashews in a blender and process until very smooth. Add the remaining 1½ cups Pistachio Milk and all of the agave syrup, almond extract, and salt and process until blended. Transfer to a jar and chill in the refrigerator for at least 2 hours or up to 2 days. Put the mixture in an ice-cream maker and freeze according to the manufacturer's directions. Crumble the finely chopped pistachios into the ice-cream maker 30 seconds before you turn the machine off.

Pistachio Ice Cream tastes best if eaten immediately, but it will keep for 5 days stored in a sealed container in the freezer. Thaw for a few minutes before serving.

ahead of time

Soak the pistachios and the cashews for 8 to 12 hours. Drain and rinse. The soaked nuts can be stored in the refrigerator for 2 days.

PISTA KULFI (Indian Pistachio Ice Cream): Replace the almond extract with 1/4 teaspoon of ground cardamom.

B

How could a fat-free ice cream so rich and creamy be made with just two ingredients?

banana-chocolate chip ice cream

YIELD: 2 CUPS (2 TO 3 SERVINGS)

INGREDIENTS

3 ripe bananas, cut into ½-inch slices

2 tablespoons raw cacao nibs (see page 4)

EQUIPMENT

cutting board

chef's knife

parchment paper (see page 9)

baking sheet or plate

measuring spoons

food processor

rubber spatula

Place the banana slices on a parchment-lined baking sheet or plate and set in the freezer for 4 to 12 hours. Put the frozen banana slices in a food processor fitted with the S blade and process until smooth. This will take a few minutes. Let the machine run until the bananas are completely smooth and creamy. Add the raw cacao nibs and process just until the nibs are broken up, about 15 seconds. Serve immediately.

ahead of time

Slice the bananas and freeze them for 4 to 12 hours.

This exotic ice cream will send coconut lovers to the tropics! Serve with Banana-Caramel Crumble *(page 47)* or Pineapple Upside-Down Cake *(page 72)*.

coconut ice cream

YIELD: 2 CUPS (4 SERVINGS)

INGREDIENTS

1½ cups young coconut meat (from 3 coconuts; see page 5)

1¼ cups water

½ cup light or dark agave syrup

2 tablespoons virgin coconut oil, melted (see page 5)

¼ teaspoon vanilla extract

⅛ teaspoon salt

½ cup unsweetened shredded dried coconut

EQUIPMENT

small saucepan

cutting board

cleaver

large spoon

measuring cups and spoons

blender

rubber spatula

jar

ice-cream maker

Place the coconut meat, water, agave syrup, coconut oil, vanilla extract, and salt in a blender and process until very smooth. Add the dried coconut and pulse briefly to mix. Transfer to a jar and chill in the refrigerator for 30 to 60 minutes. Put the mixture in an ice-cream maker and freeze according to the manufacturer's directions.

Coconut ice cream tastes best if eaten immediately, but it will keep for 5 days stored in a sealed container in the freezer. Thaw for a few minutes before serving.

B

banana split

This elaborate sundae is worth the work.

See photo facing page 24. **YIELD: 1 SERVING**

INGREDIENTS

1 ripe banana

3 scoops raw ice cream
(see note)

2 tablespoons Chocolate Ganache (page 26), warmed; **Caramel Sauce** (page 25), warmed; **and/or Raspberry Coulis** (page 23)

1 tablespoon raw almonds or walnuts (unsoaked), chopped (optional)

EQUIPMENT

cutting board

chef's knife

serving plate

ice-cream scoop

spoons or squeeze bottles

Cut the banana in half lengthwise. Place the halves side by side on a plate, forming a boat. Top with the ice cream and drizzle on the sauces with spoons or squeeze bottles. Top with the chopped nuts, if desired.

ahead of time

Soak the Brazil nuts, almonds, and cashews for 8 to 12 hours. Drain and rinse. The soaked nuts can be stored in the refrigerator for 2 days.

NOTE: For the ice creams, choose one or more of the following: Banana–Chocolate Chip Ice Cream *(page 64)*, Brazil Nut–Vanilla Ice Cream *(page 57)*, Chocolate Ice Cream *(page 59)*, Coconut Ice Cream *(page 65)*, Mint Chip Ice Cream *(page 61)*, Pistachio Ice Cream *(page 63)*, or Strawberries 'n' Cream Ice Cream *(page 58)*.

Peach Melba is traditionally made with poached fruit, but as long as your peaches are very ripe, it tastes delicious raw.

peach melba

YIELD: 1 SERVING

INGREDIENTS

1 ripe peach or nectarine, halved and pitted

2 scoops Brazil Nut–Vanilla Ice Cream (page 57)

¼ cup Raspberry Coulis (page 23)

¼ cup fresh raspberries

EQUIPMENT

cutting board

chef's knife

ice-cream scoop

measuring cups

spoon or squeeze bottle

serving plate or bowl

Cut the peach halves in half again lengthwise. Place the quarters on a serving plate or in a small bowl. Add the ice cream. Drizzle on the Raspberry Coulis with a spoon or a squeeze bottle. Top with the fresh raspberries. Serve immediately.

ahead of time

Soak the Brazil nuts and cashews for 8 to 12 hours. Drain and rinse. The soaked nuts can be stored in the refrigerator for 2 days.

Thaw the frozen raspberries in the refrigerator for 24 hours or at room temperature for 8 to 12 hours.

Purple and white make for a regal combination
of sorbet and ice cream.

blackberry sundae

See photo facing page 24.   **YIELD: 1 SERVING**

INGREDIENTS

**1 scoop Brazil Nut–
Vanilla Ice Cream**
(page 57)

**1 scoop Blackberry
Sorbet** (page 51)

**2 tablespoons Blackberry
Coulis** (page 23)

Fresh blackberries

EQUIPMENT

parfait glass or bowl

ice-cream scoop

**spoon or
squeeze bottle**

Place the Brazil Nut–Vanilla Ice Cream and Blackberry Sorbet
in a bowl or parfait glass and drizzle on the Blackberry Coulis
with a spoon or squeeze bottle. Top with fresh blackberries.

ahead of time

Soak the Brazil nuts and cashews for 8 to 12 hours. Drain and
rinse. The soaked nuts can be stored in the refrigerator for 2 days.

RASPBERRY SUNDAE: Use Raspberry Sorbet *(page 51)*, Raspberry Coulis *(page
23)*, and fresh raspberries instead of Blackberry Sorbet, Blackberry Coulis, and
fresh blackberries.

PRETTY IN PINK SUNDAE: Replace the Blackberry Sorbet with Strawberries 'n'
Cream Ice Cream *(page 58)*. Use Raspberry Coulis and fresh sliced strawberries
instead of Blackberry Coulis and fresh blackberries.

The fantasy of every kid at heart.

knockout brownie sundae

YIELD: 1 SERVING

INGREDIENTS

1 Really! One Bowl Brownie (page 83)

1 scoop Brazil Nut–Vanilla Ice Cream (page 57)

2 tablespoons Chocolate Ganache (page 26), warmed

EQUIPMENT

serving plate

brownie serving spatula

ice-cream scoop

spoon or squeeze bottle

Place the brownie on a serving plate. Preheat an oven to 200 degrees F. Turn off the oven, insert the plate, and warm the brownie for 15 minutes. Alternatively, heat the brownie in a food dehydrator at 105 degrees F for 30 minutes.

Top with the ice cream and drizzle on the Chocolate Ganache with a spoon or squeeze bottle. Serve immediately.

ahead of time

Soak the Brazil nuts and cashews for 8 to 12 hours. Drain and rinse. The soaked nuts can be stored in the refrigerator for 2 days.

Three great flavors converge in one dessert—velvety caramel, ultrarich chocolate, and nutty praline.

turtle sundae

YIELD: 1 SERVING

INGREDIENTS

2 scoops Brazil Nut–Vanilla Ice Cream (page 57)

2 tablespoons Caramel Sauce (page 25), warmed

2 tablespoons Chocolate Ganache (page 26), warmed

1 tablespoon Praline (page 28; optional)

EQUIPMENT

parfait glass or bowl

ice-cream scoop

2 spoons or squeeze bottles

Place the Brazil Nut–Vanilla Ice Cream in a bowl or parfait glass, and drizzle on the Caramel Sauce and Chocolate Ganache with spoons or squeeze bottles. Top with the Praline, if desired.

ahead of time

Soak the Brazil nuts and cashews for 8 to 12 hours. Drain and rinse. The soaked nuts can be stored in the refrigerator for 2 days.

Raw cakes, cookies, and bars are made with nuts, dried coconut, and dates and are flavored with cocoa *(Chocolate Cake with Fudge Frosting, page 74)*, fresh fruit *(Jumble Berry Upside-Down Cake and Pineapple Upside-Down Cake, page 72)*, or spices and citrus zests *(Spice Cake, page 77, and Lemon-Cranberry-Pistachio Cookies, page 80)*. Don't forget to use 6-inch pans for cakes, and 6- or 7-inch springform pans for cheesecakes, rather than the standard 8- or 9- inch versions. Smaller pans allow you to use less of each ingredient while creating impressive-looking cakes. If you wish to use an 8-inch cake pan, double the recipe. When using a 9-inch cake pan, multiply the recipe by two and a half.

For quick finger-food pastries, try Chocolate Cupcakes *(page 73)*, cookies *(pages 80–81)*, and Really! One Bowl Brownies *(page 83)*. These desserts, along with assorted candies *(pages 105–111)*, are practical for buffets, since no utensils are required.

CAKES, COOKIES, AND BARS

An upside-down cake without the ordeal of baking? Yes, and beautiful too.

jumble berry upside-down cake

See photo facing page 25.   **YIELD: ONE 6-INCH CAKE** (8 SERVINGS)

INGREDIENTS

1 cup fresh blueberries

¾ cup fresh raspberries

¾ cup sliced fresh strawberries

1 tablespoon light agave syrup

2½ cups Shortbread Crust (page 32)

EQUIPMENT

cutting board

small serrated knife

measuring cups and spoons

medium mixing bowl

rubber spatula

parchment paper

6-inch cake pan (see page 7)

kitchen scissors

Place the berries and agave syrup in a medium mixing bowl and toss to combine. Let sit for 5 minutes.

Line a 6-inch cake pan with a parchment-paper round (see page 9). Place half of the berries on the paper. Top with half of the Shortbread Crust, distributing it evenly. Press down with your hand to compact. Repeat with the remaining berries, and then cover with the remaining crust. Chill in the refrigerator for at least 30 minutes or up to 12 hours before serving.

To serve, run a knife around the edge of the pan to loosen the cake. Place a serving plate upside down on the cake pan. Invert, then lift the pan off. Remove the parchment round.

Covered with plastic wrap and stored in the refrigerator, Jumble Berry Upside-Down Cake will keep for 2 days.

STRAWBERRY UPSIDE-DOWN CAKE: Replace the mixed berries with 2½ cups of thinly sliced strawberries.

PINEAPPLE UPSIDE-DOWN CAKE: Replace the light agave syrup with dark agave syrup or maple syrup. Replace the mixed berries with 2½ cups of thinly sliced pineapple (see page 13). Serve with Avocado Crème Anglaise *(page 22)*, Coconut Ice Cream *(page 65)*, or Caramel Sauce *(page 25)*.

PINEAPPLE-CHERRY UPSIDE-DOWN CAKE: Replace 1 cup of the sliced pineapple with 1 cup of thawed frozen cherries.

It's easy to understand why cupcake shops are popping up all across the country. Who doesn't want a personal cake? Now you can enjoy the cupcake craze—without the white sugar, white flour, and butter.

chocolate cupcakes

YIELD: 12 MINI CUPCAKES (6 SERVINGS)

INGREDIENTS

1½ cups raw walnuts (unsoaked)

Pinch salt

8 pitted medjool dates

⅓ cup cocoa powder or raw cacao powder (see page 5)

½ teaspoon vanilla extract

1 teaspoon filtered water

⅓ cup Chocolate Ganache (page 26), freshly made or warmed (optional)

Unsweetened shredded dried coconut (optional)

EQUIPMENT

measuring cups and spoons

food processor

rubber spatula

mini-muffin pan (optional)

1¾ x 1-inch paper baking cups

small offset spatula

Place the walnuts and salt in a food processor fitted with the S blade and process until finely ground. Add the dates and process until the mixture begins to stick together. Add the cocoa powder and vanilla extract and process until the powder is incorporated. Add the water and process briefly.

Line a mini-muffin pan with 1¾ x 1-inch paper baking cups. (If you don't have a mini-muffin pan, place the baking cups on a plate.) Fill each baking cup with 1½ tablespoons of the chocolate mixture. Press down with your fingers to compact each cupcake. Frost with the Chocolate Ganache using a small offset spatula and/or sprinkle with dried coconut, if desired. Chill the frosted cupcakes in the refrigerator for at least 30 minutes before serving.

Covered with plastic wrap, Chocolate Cupcakes will keep for 5 days stored in the refrigerator or for 2 weeks stored in the freezer.

Dive in.

chocolate cake with fudge frosting

See photo facing page 88.   **YIELD: ONE 6-INCH CAKE** (8 SERVINGS)

INGREDIENTS

3 cups raw walnuts
(unsoaked)

⅛ teaspoon salt

16 pitted medjool dates

**⅔ cup cocoa powder
or raw cacao powder**
(see page 5)

**1 teaspoon vanilla
extract**

**2 teaspoons filtered
water**

**⅓ cup Chocolate
Ganache** (page 26),
freshly made or warmed

**Unsweetened shredded
dried coconut** (optional)

Fresh raspberries
(optional)

Place the walnuts and salt in a food processor fitted with the S blade and process until finely ground. Add the dates and process until the mixture begins to stick together. Add the cocoa powder and vanilla extract and process until the powder is incorporated. Add the water and process briefly.

Line a 6-inch cake pan with a parchment-paper round (see page 9). Pour the chocolate mixture into the pan and distribute it evenly. Press down with your hand to compact.

To serve, run a knife around the edge of the pan to loosen the cake. Place a serving plate upside down on top of the cake pan. Invert, then lift the pan off. Remove the parchment round.

**measuring cups
and spoons**

food processor

rubber spatula

parchment paper

6-inch cake pan
(see page 7)

kitchen scissors

small offset spatula

Using a small offset spatula, frost with the Chocolate Ganache, allowing some of the ganache to drizzle down the sides of the cake. Chill in the refrigerator for at least 30 minutes before serving. Garnish each serving with dried coconut and/or fresh raspberries, if desired.

Covered with plastic wrap, Chocolate Cake with Fudge Frosting will keep for 5 days stored in the refrigerator or for 2 weeks stored in the freezer.

GERMAN CHOCOLATE CAKE: Frost with ⅓ cup of Coconut-Pecan Frosting *(page 27)* instead of the Chocolate Ganache.

This moist dessert has a molten core. It's popular in restaurants yet easy to make at home. For an elegant presentation, fill a small pitcher with Vanilla Cashew Cream *(page 18)* or Raspberry Coulis *(page 23)* and pour the sauce over each cake at the table. Or, serve the cake with a side of Brazil Nut–Vanilla Ice Cream *(page 57)*, Raspberry Sorbet *(page 51)*, or Strawberry Sorbet *(page 52)*.

chocolate lava cake

YIELD: 2 SERVINGS

INGREDIENTS

1½ cups raw walnuts (unsoaked)

Pinch salt

8 pitted medjool dates

⅓ cup cocoa powder or raw cacao powder (see page 5)

½ teaspoon vanilla extract

1 teaspoon filtered water

½ cup Chocolate Ganache (page 26), freshly made or warmed

2 teaspoons unsweetened shredded dried coconut (optional)

EQUIPMENT

measuring cups and spoons

food processor

2 (6-ounce) **ramekins**

Place the walnuts and salt in a food processor fitted with the S blade and process until finely ground. Add the dates and process until the mixture begins to stick together. Add the cocoa powder and vanilla extract and process until the powder is incorporated. Add the water and process briefly.

Place ⅓ cup of the chocolate mixture in each 6-ounce ramekin and press down with your fingers to compact. Add 2 tablespoons of the Chocolate Ganache to each ramekin. Top with 2 additional tablespoons of the chocolate mixture and press down slightly. Garnish with the dried coconut, if desired.

To serve, preheat an oven to 200 degrees F. Turn off the oven, insert the ramekins, and warm for 15 minutes. Alternatively, heat the cakes in a food dehydrator at 105 degrees F for 30 minutes.

Covered with plastic wrap and stored in the refrigerator, Chocolate Lava Cake will keep for 1 week.

CHOCOLATE-CARAMEL LAVA CAKE: Replace the Chocolate Ganache with 2 tablespoons of Caramel Sauce *(page 25)*, freshly made or warmed.

This spicy cake is flavorful enough to serve unadorned, but it's also great with Vanilla Cashew Cream *(page 18)*, Chocolate Cashew Cream *(page 19)*, Caramel Sauce *(page 25)*, or Winter Fruit Compote *(page 42)*.

spice cake

YIELD: ONE 6-INCH CAKE (8 SERVINGS)

INGREDIENTS

½ cup raw almonds
(unsoaked)

½ cup unsweetened shredded dried coconut

1 teaspoon ground cinnamon

½ teaspoon ground ginger

¼ teaspoon salt

¼ teaspoon ground cloves

Pinch ground nutmeg

1 cup raw walnuts
(unsoaked)

1 cup raw pecans
(unsoaked)

8 pitted medjool dates

1 teaspoon orange zest
(see page 8)

½ cup raisins

1 tablespoon maple syrup or dark agave syrup

EQUIPMENT

measuring cups and spoons

file grater or zester

food processor

rubber spatula

parchment paper

6-inch cake pan
(see page 7)

kitchen scissors

Place the almonds, coconut, cinnamon, ginger, salt, cloves, and nutmeg in a food processor fitted with the S blade and process until finely ground. Add the walnuts and pecans and process until finely ground. Add the dates and orange zest and process until the mixture begins to stick together. Add the raisins and maple syrup and process briefly to incorporate.

Line a 6-inch cake pan with a parchment-paper round (see page 9). Pour the nut mixture into the pan and distribute it evenly. Press down with your hand to compact.

To serve, run a knife around the edge of the pan to loosen the cake. Place a serving plate upside down on top of the cake pan. Invert, then lift the pan off. Remove the parchment round.

Covered with plastic wrap, Spice Cake will keep for 5 days stored in the refrigerator or for 2 weeks stored in the freezer.

CARROT CAKE: Add 1/2 cup grated carrots to the food processor along with the dates and the orange zest.

R

Traditional cheesecake relies on multiple dairy products: cream cheese, cottage cheese, and sour cream. You won't miss them in my wickedly-rich version.

red, white, and blue cheesecake

INGREDIENTS

CRUST:

1 cup raw walnuts (unsoaked)

¼ cup unsweetened shredded dried coconut

¼ cup whole cane sugar (see page 6)

Pinch salt

¼ cup raisins

4 pitted medjool dates

FILLING:

1 cup raw cashews, soaked for 8 to 12 hours (1¼ cups after soaking), drained and rinsed

½ cup young coconut meat (from 1 coconut; see page 5)

½ cup freshly squeezed lemon juice

½ cup light agave syrup

¼ cup Date Paste (page 17)

⅛ teaspoon salt

½ cup virgin coconut oil, melted (see page 5)

1 tablespoon soy lecithin powder (see page 6; optional)

BERRY TOPPING:

1 cup fresh blueberries

½ cup fresh raspberries

½ cup sliced fresh strawberries

To make the crust, place the walnuts, coconut, sugar, and salt in a food processor fitted with the S blade. Process until finely ground. Add the raisins and dates and process until the coarse crumbs begin to stick together. Press into a 6- or 7-inch spring-form pan.

To make the filling, place the cashews, coconut meat, lemon juice, agave syrup, Date Paste, and salt in a blender and process until very smooth. Stop occasionally to scrape down the sides of the blender jar with a rubber spatula. Add the coconut oil and optional soy lecithin powder and process until blended. Pour the filling into the crust and spread it evenly with a small offset spatula.

Scatter the blueberries, raspberries, and strawberries on top of the cheesecake and press them in slightly. Chill in the refrigerator for at least 2 hours before serving.

**measuring cups
and spoons**

food processor

rubber spatula

blender

citrus juicer or reamer

small saucepan

cleaver

large spoon

**6- or 7-inch springform
pan** (see page 7)

small offset spatula

Covered with plastic wrap and stored in the refrigerator, Red, White, and Blue Cheesecake will keep for 5 days.

ahead of time

Soak the cashews for 8 to 12 hours. Drain and rinse. Soaked cashews can be stored in the refrigerator for 2 days.

STRAWBERRY CHEESECAKE: Replace the mixed berries with 2 of cups sliced fresh strawberries. Arrange the strawberries attractively on top of the cheesecake. Serve with a small pitcher of Strawberry Soup (page 35) to drizzle over each cheesecake slice at the table.

CHEESECAKE WITH CONCORD GRAPE SORBET: Omit the berry topping and serve each slice of cheesecake with a scoop of Concord Grape Sorbet *(page 53)*.

These nutty cookies, punctuated by bright red, tart cranberries, will light up any holiday party.

lemon-cranberry-pistachio cookies

YIELD: 24 COOKIES

INGREDIENTS

1 cup raw almonds
(unsoaked)

¼ cup raw pistachios
(unsoaked)

Pinch salt

8 pitted medjool dates

1 teaspoon lemon zest
(see page 8)

¼ cup dried cranberries

EQUIPMENT

**measuring cups
and spoons**

food processor

rubber spatula

small mixing bowl

medium mixing bowl

file grater or zester

plate

Place ½ cup of the almonds in a food processor fitted with the S blade and process until finely ground. Set aside in a small mixing bowl.

Put the remaining ½ cup of almonds and all of the pistachios and salt in the food processor and process until coarsely chopped. Add the dates and lemon zest and process until the mixture begins to stick together. Don't overprocess; chunks of almonds and pistachios should still be visible. Add the dried cranberries and pulse briefly, just until mixed.

Remove the cookie dough from the food processor and place in a medium mixing bowl. Scoop about 1 tablespoon of the dough into your hand and squeeze it firmly until it sticks together. Roll it into a 1-inch ball and flatten it slightly to make a cookie. Repeat until all of the dough has been used. Roll each cookie in the ground almonds and place it on a plate. Chill the cookies in the refrigerator for at least 1 hour before serving.

Stored in a sealed container, Lemon-Cranberry-Pistachio Cookies will keep for 1 month in the refrigerator or for 3 months in the freezer.

Sweet, chewy, and gingery—America's favorite spice cookie goes raw.

ginger spice cookies

YIELD: 24 COOKIES

INGREDIENTS

1 cup raw almonds (unsoaked)

¼ cup raw walnuts (unsoaked)

2 tablespoons whole cane sugar (see page 6)

½ teaspoon ground ginger

¼ teaspoon ground cinnamon

Pinch salt

Pinch ground nutmeg

8 pitted medjool dates

¼ cup raisins

EQUIPMENT

measuring cups and spoons

food processor

rubber spatula

small mixing bowl

medium mixing bowl

plate

Place ½ cup of the almonds in a food processor fitted with the S blade and process until finely ground. Set aside in a small mixing bowl.

Put the remaining ½ cup of almonds and all of the walnuts, sugar, ginger, cinnamon, salt, and nutmeg in the food processor and process until coarsely chopped. Add the dates and process until the mixture begins to stick together. Don't overprocess; chunks of almonds and walnuts should still be visible. Add the raisins and pulse briefly, just until mixed.

Remove the cookie dough from the food processor and place it in a medium mixing bowl. Scoop about 1 tablespoon of the dough into your hand and squeeze it firmly until it sticks together. Roll it into a 1-inch ball and flatten it slightly to make a cookie. Repeat until all of the dough has been used. Roll each cookie in the ground almonds and place on a plate. Chill in the refrigerator for at least 1 hour before serving.

Stored in a sealed container, Ginger Spice Cookies will keep for 1 month in the refrigerator or for 3 months in the freezer.

R raspberry squares

If you like buttery shortbread cookies and sweet-tart raspberry jam, you'll love them combined in this handsome bar. Raspberry Squares require only pantry ingredients, so they're perfect for a last-minute dessert.

YIELD: 8 SQUARES (8 SERVINGS)

INGREDIENTS

2½ cups Shortbread Crust (page 32)

¾ cup Raspberry Jam (page 24)

EQUIPMENT

measuring cups

8-inch glass baking dish

rubber spatula

Set aside ¼ cup of the Shortbread Crust. Pour the remaining 2¼ cups of crust into an 8-inch glass baking dish and distribute it evenly. Press down firmly with your hand to compact. Spread the Raspberry Jam evenly over the crust with a rubber spatula. Sprinkle the remaining ¼ cup of crust on top of the jam. Chill in the refrigerator for at least 2 hours before serving. Cut into squares.

Covered with plastic wrap and stored in the refrigerator, Raspberry Squares will keep for 5 days.

Ten minutes is all it takes.

really! one bowl brownies

YIELD: 16 SMALL BROWNIES (8 SERVINGS)

3 cups raw walnuts
(unsoaked)

⅛ teaspoon salt

16 pitted medjool dates

**⅔ cup cocoa powder
or raw cacao powder**
(see page 5)

**½ cup dried cherries,
chopped**

¼ cup raw cacao nibs
(see page 4; optional)

**2 teaspoons filtered
water**

EQUIPMENT

**measuring cups
and spoons**

food processor

small mixing bowl

8-inch glass baking dish

Place the walnuts in a food processor fitted with the S blade and process until coarsely chopped. Remove ½ cup of the walnuts and set aside in a small mixing bowl. Add the salt to the food processor and process until the walnuts are finely ground. Add the dates and process until the mixture begins to stick together. Add the cocoa powder and process to incorporate. Add the chopped walnuts, dried cherries, optional cacao nibs, and water and process briefly, just until mixed.

Pour the mixture evenly into an 8-inch glass baking dish and press down with your hand to compact. Cut into squares.

Covered with plastic wrap, Really! One Bowl Brownies will keep for 5 days stored in the refrigerator or for 2 weeks stored in the freezer.

BROWNIES WITH FUDGE FROSTING: Frost the brownies with ⅓ cup of Chocolate Ganache *(page 26)*, freshly made or warmed. Chill in the refrigerator for at least 30 minutes before serving.

*R*aw pies and tarts are easier to make than baked versions and are better for you. The crusts take ten minutes to prepare and will keep in the freezer for months. Just process the ingredients in a food processor and press the mixture into a pan—no rolling or baking required! Ground nuts and dried coconut replace flour and butter, and a few dates bind the crust together. With slight variations, you can create Shortbread Crust *(page 32)*, Graham Crust *(page 31)*, Almond-Pecan Crust *(page 29)*, and Chocolate Cookie Crust *(page 30)*. Creamy pie fillings are made with avocado, as in Key Lime Tart *(page 87)* and Chocolate Cream Pie *(page 93)*, or with young coconut, for Classic Fresh Fruit Tart *(page 92)*, Lemon Tart *(page 86)*, and Banana Cream Pie *(page 89)*.

Tarts look fancier than pies, but they're easy to form, since the tart pan is fluted. (Make sure your pans have removable bottoms.) Moreover, any tart recipe can be made into tartlets. Just use six (4½-inch) tartlet pans, or halve the recipe and make three tartlets.

For an elegant presentation of individual slices of pie or tart, drizzle the serving plates with Vanilla Cashew Cream *(page 18)*, Raspberry Coulis *(page 23)*, or Chocolate Ganache *(page 26)*. For easy drizzling, transfer the sauce to a squeeze bottle. (To fill the bottle, pour the sauce into a zipper-lock plastic bag, cut off a tip, and squeeze the contents into the bottle.) Create a lattice-top pie by squeezing Vanilla Cashew Cream in a criss-cross pattern. This looks beautiful—especially on Pumpkin Pie *(page 96)*.

PIES AND TARTS

Creamy, light lemon curd pairs with a buttery shortbread crust in this French classic.

lemon tart

INGREDIENTS

2½ cups Shortbread Crust (page 32)

2 cups Lemon Curd (page 21)

Fresh blueberries, raspberries, or sliced strawberries (optional)

EQUIPMENT

9-inch tart pan with removable bottom

small offset spatula

Pour the crust crumbs into the tart pan. Use a light circular motion with your palm and fingers to distribute the crumbs uniformly along the bottom. Gently push some of the crumbs up the sides of the pan to the rim in order to create a ¼-inch-thick, loosely packed wall. Next, press the crust on the bottom of the pan down with your fingers and palm (be especially firm where the bottom of the pan joins the sides). To finish, press with your thumb to consolidate the crust wall along the pan's sides.

Pour the Lemon Curd into the crust, spreading it evenly with a small offset spatula. Chill in the refrigerator for at least 2 hours before serving. Decorate the tart with blueberries, raspberries, or sliced strawberries, if desired.

Covered with plastic wrap and stored in the refrigerator, Lemon Tart will keep for 3 days.

ORANGE TART: Replace the Lemon Curd with Orange Curd *(page 21)*. Decorate the tart with the segments of 4 navel oranges. Alternatively, serve tart slices with Macerated Citrus *(page 38)* or Classic Ambrosia *(page 39)*.

Traditionally, this all-American dessert includes sweetened condensed milk and egg yolks—artery cloggers you won't miss in my decadent raw version.

key lime tart

YIELD: ONE 9-INCH TART (8 SERVINGS)

INGREDIENTS

2½ cups Shortbread Crust (page 32), **or 2 cups Graham Crust** (page 31)

3 cups Key Lime Pots de Crème (page 104)

Fresh raspberries (optional)

EQUIPMENT

9-inch tart pan with removable bottom

small offset spatula

Pour the crust crumbs into the tart pan. Use a light circular motion with your palm and fingers to distribute the crumbs uniformly along the bottom. Gently push some of the crumbs up the sides of the pan to the rim in order to create a ¼-inch-thick, loosely packed wall. Next, press the crust on the bottom of the pan down with your fingers and palm (be especially firm where the bottom of the pan joins the sides). To finish, press with your thumb to consolidate the crust wall along the pan's sides.

Pour the Key Lime Pots de Crème into the crust, spreading it evenly with a small offset spatula. Chill in the refrigerator for at least 2 hours before serving. Decorate the tart with raspberries, if desired.

Covered with plastic wrap and stored in the refrigerator, Key Lime Tart will keep for 3 days.

This cloudlike pie is heaven for coconut lovers. My Chocolate Cookie Crust complements the filling perfectly and makes a beautiful black-and-white presentation.

coconut cream pie with chocolate cookie crust

YIELD: ONE 9-INCH PIE (8 SERVINGS)

INGREDIENTS

2 cups Chocolate Cookie Crust (page 30)

2 cups young coconut meat (from 4 coconuts; see page 5)

½ cup coconut water

½ cup light agave syrup

⅛ teaspoon salt

3 tablespoons virgin coconut oil, melted (see page 5)

1 tablespoon soy lecithin powder (see page 6; optional)

1⅓ cups unsweetened shredded dried coconut

½ cup Chocolate Ganache (page 26), freshly made or warmed (optional)

EQUIPMENT

measuring cups and spoons

small saucepan

cutting board

cleaver

large spoon

9-inch pie pan

blender

small offset spatula

Pour the crust crumbs into the pie pan. Use a light circular motion with your palm and fingers to distribute the crumbs uniformly along the bottom. Gently push some of the crumbs up the sides of the pan to the rim in order to create a ¼-inch-thick, loosely packed wall. Next, press the crust on the bottom of the pan down with your fingers and palm (be especially firm where the bottom of the pan joins the sides). To finish, press with your thumb to consolidate the crust wall along the pan's sides.

Place the coconut meat, coconut water, agave syrup, and salt in a blender and process until smooth. Add the coconut oil and optional soy lecithin powder and process until blended. Add 1 cup of the dried coconut and pulse briefly to mix. Pour the coconut mixture into the crust, spreading it evenly with a small offset spatula. Distribute the remaining ⅓ cup dried coconut over the top of the pie. Chill in the refrigerator for at least 2 hours before serving.

Serve chilled or at room temperature. Drizzle with the Chocolate Ganache, if desired.

Covered with plastic wrap and stored in the refrigerator, Coconut Cream Pie will keep for 3 days.

chocolate cake with fudge frosting, page 74

counterclockwise from top: greek dates, page 110, dark chocolate truffles, page 106,
blondie cashew freezer fudge, page 108, chocolate candy cups, page 109

Each bite of this pie delights with its harmony of textures and flavors—crumbly crust, creamy vanilla custard, and ripe bananas.

banana cream pie

YIELD: ONE 9-INCH PIE (8 SERVINGS)

INGREDIENTS

2 cups Graham Crust
(page 31)

2 ripe bananas

2 cups Pastry Cream
(page 20)

EQUIPMENT

9-inch pie pan

chef's knife

cutting board

small offset spatula

Pour the crust crumbs into the pie pan. Use a light circular motion with your palm and fingers to distribute the crumbs uniformly along the bottom. Gently push some of the crumbs up the sides of the pan to the rim in order to create a $1/4$-inch-thick, loosely packed wall. Next, press the crust on the bottom of the pan down with your fingers and palm (be especially firm where the bottom of the pan joins the sides). To finish, press with your thumb to consolidate the crust wall along the pan's sides.

Cut each banana crosswise into 3 pieces; then thinly slice each piece lengthwise. Layer the banana slices all over the bottom of the crust.

Pour the Pastry Cream over the bananas, spreading it evenly with a small offset spatula. Chill in the refrigerator for at least 2 hours before serving.

Covered with plastic wrap and stored in the refrigerator, Banana Cream Pie will keep for 3 days.

Try this tart after an Asian or Latin American meal.

tropical ambrosia tart

YIELD: ONE 9-INCH TART (8 SERVINGS)

INGREDIENTS

2½ cups Shortbread Crust (page 32)

2 cups Tropical Ambrosia (page 40)

EQUIPMENT

9-inch tart pan with removable bottom

small offset spatula

Pour the crust crumbs into the tart pan. Use a light circular motion with your palm and fingers to distribute the crumbs uniformly along the bottom. Gently push some of the crumbs up the sides of the pan to the rim in order to create a ¼-inch-thick, loosely packed wall. Next, press the crust on the bottom of the pan down with your fingers and palm (be especially firm where the bottom of the pan joins the sides). To finish, press with your thumb to consolidate the crust wall along the pan's sides.

Pour the Tropical Ambrosia into the crust, spreading it evenly with a small offset spatula. Chill in the refrigerator for at least 2 hours before serving.

Covered with plastic wrap and stored in the refrigerator, Tropical Ambrosia Tart will keep for 3 days.

Three contrasting textures combine beautifully in this tart—silky vanilla custard, chewy tart-sweet cherries, and crunchy almonds.

cherry custard tart with sliced almonds

YIELD: ONE 9-INCH TART (8 SERVINGS)

INGREDIENTS

2½ cups Shortbread Crust (page 32)

2 cups Pastry Cream (page 20)

1 (10-ounce) **package frozen cherries,** thawed and drained (1½ cups)

¾ cup sliced raw almonds

EQUIPMENT

medium mixing bowl

strainer or colander

9-inch tart pan with removable bottom

small offset spatula

Pour the crust crumbs into the tart pan. Use a light circular motion with your palm and fingers to distribute the crumbs uniformly along the bottom. Gently push some of the crumbs up the sides of the pan to the rim in order to create a ¼-inch-thick, loosely packed wall. Next, press the crust on the bottom of the pan down with your fingers and palm (be especially firm where the bottom of the pan joins the sides). To finish, press with your thumb to consolidate the crust wall along the pan's sides.

Pour the Pastry Cream into the crust, spreading it evenly with a small offset spatula. Place the cherries on the cream and press them in slightly. Scatter the almonds on top. Chill in the refrigerator for at least 2 hours before serving.

Covered with plastic wrap and stored in the refrigerator, Cherry Custard Tart with Sliced Almonds will keep for 2 days.

ahead of time

Thaw the frozen cherries in the refrigerator for 24 hours or at room temperature for 8 to 12 hours.

This elegant pastry (think bakery windows in Paris) tastes as good as it looks.

classic fresh fruit tart

See photo between pages 56 and 57.   **YIELD: ONE 9-INCH TART** (8 SERVINGS)

INGREDIENTS

2½ cups Shortbread Crust (page 32)

2 cups Pastry Cream (page 20)

1 kiwifruit, peeled and sliced into half-moons

½ cup fresh blueberries

½ cup fresh blackberries

½ cup sliced fresh strawberries

EQUIPMENT

medium mixing bowl

9-inch tart pan with removable bottom

small offset spatula

cutting board

small serrated knife

Pour the crust crumbs into the tart pan. Use a light circular motion with your palm and fingers to distribute the crumbs uniformly along the bottom. Gently push some of the crumbs up the sides of the pan to the rim in order to create a $1/4$-inch-thick, loosely packed wall. Next, press the crust on the bottom of the pan down with your fingers and palm (be especially firm where the bottom of the pan joins the sides). To finish, press with your thumb to consolidate the crust wall along the pan's sides.

Pour the Pastry Cream into the crust, spreading it evenly with a small offset spatula. Arrange the fruit in concentric circles, beginning with the kiwifruit half-moons in the center of the tart, moving outward with circles of blueberries and blackberries, and ending with the sliced strawberries around the edges. Chill in the refrigerator for at least 2 hours before serving.

Covered with plastic wrap and stored in the refrigerator, Classic Fresh Fruit Tart will keep for 2 days.

RASPBERRY TART: Top the tart with 2 cups of fresh raspberries instead of the other fruits.

Celebrate life's bittersweet moments (or, actually, any moment) with this bittersweet pie. Serve it topped with Vanilla Cashew Cream *(page 18)* or Chocolate Cashew Cream *(page 19)*.

chocolate cream pie

YIELD: ONE 9-INCH PIE (8 SERVINGS)

INGREDIENTS

2½ cups Shortbread Crust (page 32) **or Chocolate Cookie Crust** (page 30), **or 2 cups Graham Crust** (page 31)

2 cups Chocolate Pots de Crème (page 102)

EQUIPMENT

9-inch pie pan

small offset spatula

Pour the crust crumbs into the pie pan. Use a light circular motion with your palm and fingers to distribute the crumbs uniformly along the bottom. Gently push some of the crumbs up the sides of the pan to the rim in order to create a ¼-inch-thick, loosely packed wall. Next, press the crust on the bottom of the pan down with your fingers and palm (be especially firm where the bottom of the pan joins the sides). To finish, press with your thumb to consolidate the crust wall along the pan's sides.

Pour the Chocolate Pots de Crème into the crust, spreading it evenly with a small offset spatula. Chill in the refrigerator for at least 2 hours before serving.

Covered with plastic wrap and stored in the refrigerator, Chocolate Cream Pie will keep for 5 days.

CHOCOLATE-COCONUT FANTASY PIE: Top the pie with ½ cup of unsweetened shredded dried coconut.

My ultrarich Chocolate Truffle Tart borders on candy. For contrasting color and flavor, serve it with fresh raspberries, on a pool of Raspberry Coulis *(page 23)*, or with a side of Strawberry Sorbet *(page 52)* or Raspberry Sorbet *(page 51)*.

chocolate truffle tart

YIELD: ONE 9-INCH TART (8 SERVINGS)

INGREDIENTS

2½ cups Shortbread Crust (page 32) **or Chocolate Cookie Crust** (page 30)

1½ cups cocoa powder or raw cacao powder (see page 5)

1½ cups dark agave syrup or maple syrup

⅔ cup virgin coconut oil, melted (see page 5)

¼ teaspoon plus a pinch salt

Fresh raspberries (optional)

EQUIPMENT

measuring cups and spoons

small saucepan

blender

rubber spatula

9-inch tart pan with removable bottom

small offset spatula

Pour the crust crumbs into the tart pan. Use a light circular motion with your palm and fingers to distribute the crumbs uniformly along the bottom. Gently push some of the crumbs up the sides of the pan to the rim in order to create a ¼-inch-thick, loosely packed wall. Next, press the crust on the bottom of the pan down with your fingers and palm (be especially firm where the bottom of the pan joins the sides). To finish, press with your thumb to consolidate the crust wall along the pan's sides.

Place the cocoa powder, agave syrup, coconut oil, and salt in a blender and process until smooth. Stop occasionally to scrape down the sides of the blender jar with a rubber spatula. Pour the chocolate mixture into the crust, spreading it evenly with a small offset spatula. Chill in the refrigerator for at least 2 hours before serving. Garnish with fresh raspberries, if desired.

Covered with plastic wrap and stored in the refrigerator, Chocolate Truffle Tart will keep for 5 days.

BANANA-CHOCOLATE TARTLETS WITH CARAMEL SAUCE: Thinly slice 2 ripe bananas. Press the Shortbread Crust evenly into 6 (4½-inch) tartlet pans with removable bottoms and fill with the blended chocolate mixture. Top each tartlet with the banana slices and drizzle with Caramel Sauce *(page 25)*.

Gooey, sweet pecan pie is always a favorite for the holidays—and adding deep dark chocolate takes it right over the top.

chocolate pecan pie

YIELD: ONE 9-INCH PIE (8 SERVINGS)

INGREDIENTS

¾ cup water

½ teaspoon agar flakes (see page 4)

1 cup Date Paste (page 17)

1 tablespoon dark agave syrup or maple syrup

1 teaspoon vanilla extract

⅛ teaspoon salt

2 cups Almond-Pecan Crust (page 29)

¾ cup Chocolate Ganache (page 26), freshly made or warmed

1¼ cups raw pecans (unsoaked), chopped

EQUIPMENT

cutting board

chef's knife

9-inch pie pan

measuring cups and spoons

small saucepan

whisk

food processor

rubber spatula

small offset spatula

Place the water and agar flakes in a small saucepan on the stove and let soak for 5 to 10 minutes. Bring to a boil, lower the heat, and simmer for 5 minutes, whisking occasionally. Remove from the heat and cool slightly.

Place the Date Paste, agave syrup, vanilla extract, and salt in a food processor fitted with the S blade and process until smooth. Add the agar mixture and process until blended.

Pour the crust crumbs into the pie pan. Use a light circular motion with your palm and fingers to distribute the crumbs uniformly along the bottom. Gently push some of the crumbs up the sides of the pan to the rim in order to create a ¼-inch-thick, loosely packed wall. Next, press the crust on the bottom of the pan down with your fingers and palm (be especially firm where the bottom of the pan joins the sides). To finish, press with your thumb to consolidate the crust wall along the pan's sides.

Pour the Chocolate Ganache into the crust, spreading it evenly with a small offset spatula. Scatter ¾ cup of the pecans over the ganache. Press down lightly with your hand. Spread the date mixture evenly over the pecans with the offset spatula. Scatter the remaining ½ cup pecans on top, pressing them down slightly. Chill in the refrigerator for at least 2 hours before serving.

Covered with plastic wrap and stored in the refrigerator, Chocolate Pecan Pie will keep for 5 days.

This I-can't-believe-it's-not-cooked recipe will wow your family and friends during the Thanksgiving season. Carrots replace pumpkin because they are sweeter raw. Serve the pie with Vanilla Cashew Cream (*page 18*).

pumpkin pie

See photo facing page 57.   **YIELD: ONE 9-INCH PIE** (8 SERVINGS)

INGREDIENTS

2 cups Graham Crust
(page 31)

1½ cups water

2 teaspoons agar flakes
(see page 4)

2 cups sliced carrots

¼ cup whole cane sugar
(see page 6)

**¼ cup maple syrup
or dark agave syrup**

**2 teaspoons pumpkin
pie spice**

**1 teaspoon freshly
squeezed lemon juice**

¼ teaspoon salt

½ cup mashed avocado
(1 avocado)

Pour the crust crumbs into the pie pan. Use a light circular motion with your palm and fingers to distribute the crumbs uniformly along the bottom. Gently push some of the crumbs up the sides of the pan to the rim in order to create a ¼-inch-thick, loosely packed wall. Next, press the crust on the bottom of the pan down with your fingers and palm (be especially firm where the bottom of the pan joins the sides). To finish, press with your thumb to consolidate the crust wall along the pan's sides.

Place ¾ cup of the water and all of the agar flakes in a small saucepan on the stove. Let soak for 5 to 10 minutes. Bring to a boil, lower the heat, and simmer for 5 minutes, whisking occasionally. Remove from the heat and cool slightly.

Place the carrots, sugar, maple syrup, pumpkin pie spice, lemon juice, salt, and remaining ¾ cup water in a blender and process until smooth. Stop occasionally to scrape down the sides of the blender jar with a rubber spatula. Add the avocado and the agar mixture and process until smooth. Pour the mixture into the crust, spreading it evenly with a small offset spatula. Chill in the refrigerator for at least 2 hours before serving.

9-inch pie pan

measuring cups
and spoons

small saucepan

whisk

cutting board

chef's knife

citrus juicer or reamer

blender

rubber spatula

small mixing bowl

small offset spatula

Covered with plastic wrap and stored in the refrigerator, Pumpkin Pie will keep for 5 days.

PUMPKIN FLAN: Place 2 teaspoons of maple syrup or dark agave syrup in the bottoms of six (6-ounce) ramekins or custard cups. Pour the blended carrot mixture equally into the ramekins, spreading it evenly with a small offset spatula. Chill in the refrigerator for at least 2 hours before serving.

To serve, loosen the custard from the sides of the ramekins with a butter knife or small offset spatula. Place a small plate on top of each ramekin and invert to unmold. Yield: 6 servings.

Traditionally, this holiday pie features minced beef (not too appetizing!). My vegetarian version tastes damn good, especially when topped with Brazil Nut–Vanilla Ice Cream *(page 57)* or Vanilla Cashew Cream *(page 18)*.

M mince pie

YIELD: ONE 9-INCH PIE (8 SERVINGS)

INGREDIENTS

2½ cups Shortbread Crust (page 32)

2½ cups Winter Fruit Compote (page 42)

EQUIPMENT

9-inch pie pan

measuring cups and spoons

rubber spatula

Pour the crust crumbs into the pie pan. Use a light circular motion with your palm and fingers to distribute the crumbs uniformly along the bottom. Gently push some of the crumbs up the sides of the pan to the rim in order to create a ¼-inch-thick, loosely packed wall. Next, press the crust on the bottom of the pan down with your fingers and palm (be especially firm where the bottom of the pan joins the sides). To finish, press with your thumb to consolidate the crust wall along the pan's sides.

Pour the Winter Fruit Compote into the crust, spreading it evenly with a rubber spatula. Serve at room temperature or chilled.

Covered with plastic wrap and stored in the refrigerator, Mince Pie will keep for 5 days.

NOTE: If you prefer the pie warm, preheat an oven to 200 degrees F. Turn off the oven, insert the pie, and warm it for 15 minutes. Alternatively, heat the pie in a food dehydrator at 105 degrees F for 30 minutes.

*I*f you love soft, melt-in-your-mouth custards, you can
have this pleasure and still eat dairy free. Avocado readily
replaces cream in luxurious Chocolate Pots de Crème
(page 102) and Key Lime Pots de Crème *(page 104)*. Young coconut
meat is an excellent alternative to milk in Kheer *(page 100)* and Milk
Chocolate Pudding *(page 103)*. Vanilla Bean Crème Brulée *(page 101)*,
a restaurant favorite, is actually easier to make raw than cooked. (You
can cheat and caramelize the top.) All these creamy delights look
beautiful served in ramekins, custard cups, or shallow, fluted dishes.

CREAMY DESSERTS

Kheer, a creamy rice pudding delicately flavored with sweet spices and golden raisins, is my favorite Indian dessert. The traditional rice and milk are replaced with coconut in this raw recipe.

kheer

YIELD: 2 CUPS (4 SERVINGS)

INGREDIENTS

1 cup young coconut meat (from 2 coconuts; see page 5)

¾ cup coconut water

¼ cup light agave syrup

¼ cup unsweetened shredded dried coconut

2½ tablespoons golden raisins, soaked for 10 minutes, drained, and rinsed

1 tablespoon raw pistachios (unsoaked), chopped

½ teaspoon rose water (see page 6; optional)

¼ teaspoon ground cardamom

EQUIPMENT

cutting board

cleaver

large spoon

measuring cups and spoons

blender

rubber spatula

small mixing bowl

Place the coconut meat, coconut water, and agave syrup in a blender and process until very smooth. Stop occasionally to scrape down the sides of the blender jar with a rubber spatula. Transfer the mixture to a small mixing bowl and add the dried coconut, raisins, pistachios, rosewater, and cardamom. Stir with a rubber spatula to combine. Chill in the refrigerator for at least 2 hours before serving.

Stored in a sealed container in the refrigerator, Kheer will keep for 3 days.

V

For a traditional (not raw) burnt-cream taste, use a kitchen torch to melt the sugar on top.

vanilla bean crème brulée

YIELD: FOUR 4-OUNCE SERVINGS

INGREDIENTS

1 cup young coconut meat (from 2 coconuts; see page 5)

¼ cup filtered water

3 tablespoons light agave syrup

1 teaspoon vanilla extract

1 vanilla bean, seeds only (see page 6)

Pinch salt

Pinch turmeric

1 tablespoon virgin coconut oil, melted (see page 5)

1½ teaspoons soy lecithin powder (see page 6; optional)

⅓ cup whole cane sugar (see page 6)

EQUIPMENT

small saucepan

cutting board

cleaver

large spoon

paring knife

measuring cups and spoons

blender

rubber spatula

4 (4-ounce) **shallow, fluted dishes**

kitchen butane torch (see page 8; optional)

Place the coconut meat, water, agave syrup, vanilla extract, vanilla bean seeds, salt, and turmeric in a blender and process until very smooth. Add the coconut oil and optional soy lecithin powder and process until smooth.

Pour the mixture into shallow, fluted dishes. Chill in the refrigerator for 4 to 12 hours before serving. (Covered with plastic wrap, the custards will keep in the refrigerator for up to three days.)

Just before serving, sprinkle the top of each custard with 1½ teaspoons of the sugar. Tilt and tap each dish to remove any excess. For a traditional crème brulée, use a kitchen butane torch to melt the sugar. Keep the flame about 2 inches above the dish, until the sugar is bubbly and golden brown.

MINT CRÈME BRULÉE: Omit the vanilla bean seeds and turmeric. Put 2 tablespoons of minced fresh mint leaves into the blender along with the coconut meat, water, agave syrup, vanilla extract, and salt.

Avocados are the secret to this rich, not-too-sweet custard. Serve this versatile chocolate cream in various ways: plain; as the filling for Chocolate Cream Pie *(page 93)*; or topped with Vanilla Cashew Cream *(page 18)*, Chocolate Cashew Cream *(page 19)*, or a Dark Chocolate Truffle *(page 106)*.

chocolate pots de crème

YIELD: 2½ CUPS (6 SERVINGS)

INGREDIENTS

½ cup Date Paste (page 17)

½ cup dark agave syrup

1 tablespoon vanilla extract

⅛ teaspoon salt

1½ cups mashed avocado (3 avocados)

¾ cup cocoa powder or raw cacao powder (see page 5)

1 tablespoon virgin coconut oil, melted (see page 5)

EQUIPMENT

small saucepan

measuring cups and spoons

cutting board

chef's knife

fork or whisk

tablespoon

medium mixing bowl

food processor

rubber spatula

6 (6-ounce) **ramekins, custard cups, or coffee cups**

small offset spatula

Place the Date Paste, agave syrup, vanilla extract, and salt in a food processor fitted with the S blade and process until smooth. Add the avocado and process until blended. Stop occasionally to scrape down the sides of the work bowl with a rubber spatula. Add the cocoa powder and coconut oil and process until fully incorporated.

Pour the blended mixture evenly into 6 (6-ounce) ramekins, custard cups, or coffee cups, spreading it with a small offset spatula. Chill in the refrigerator for at least 2 hours before serving.

Covered with plastic wrap and stored in the refrigerator, Chocolate Pots de Crème will keep for 5 days.

This is the perfect pudding for those who like their chocolate milky and gentle.

*M*milk chocolate pudding

YIELD: 3 CUPS (4 TO 6 SERVINGS)

INGREDIENTS

1½ cups young coconut meat (from 3 coconuts; see page 5)

1 cup water

½ cup cocoa powder or raw cacao powder (see page 5)

½ cup light agave syrup

1 teaspoon vanilla extract

⅛ teaspoon salt

EQUIPMENT

cutting board

cleaver

large spoon

measuring cups and spoons

blender

rubber spatula

Place all of the ingredients in a blender and process until very smooth. Chill in the refrigerator for at least 2 hours before serving.

Stored in a sealed container in the refrigerator, Milk Chocolate Pudding will keep for 1 week.

BANANA–MILK CHOCOLATE PUDDING: Place half of the Milk Chocolate Pudding in an 8-inch glass baking dish and spread it evenly with a rubber spatula. Thinly slice 2 ripe bananas crosswise. Distribute the slices and 1 cup Graham Crust *(page 31)* or Shortbread Crust *(page 32)* over the pudding. Spread the remaining Milk Chocolate Pudding on top. Yield: 8 servings.

Key lime pie without the crust is a good excuse
to show off your pretty ramekins!

key lime pots de crème

YIELD: 3 CUPS (6 SERVINGS)

INGREDIENTS

1½ cups mashed avocado (3 avocados)

¾ cup freshly squeezed lime juice

¾ cup light agave syrup

⅛ teaspoon salt

½ cup virgin coconut oil, melted (see page 5)

2 tablespoons soy lecithin powder (see page 6; optional)

Fresh raspberries (optional)

EQUIPMENT

medium mixing bowl

fork or whisk

tablespoon

measuring cups and spoons

citrus juicer or reamer

small saucepan

blender

rubber spatula

6 (6-ounce) **ramekins or custard cups**

small offset spatula

Place the avocado, lime juice, agave syrup, and salt in a blender and process until smooth. Add the coconut oil and optional soy lecithin powder and process until blended. Spoon the mixture evenly into 6 (6-ounce) ramekins or custard cups. Chill in the refrigerator for at least 2 hours before serving. Garnish with fresh raspberries, if desired.

Covered with plastic wrap and stored in the refrigerator, Key Lime Pots de Crème will keep for 3 days.

All too often we satisfy our sweet tooth with store-bought candy bars—addictive, nutritionally empty, and loaded with sugar, corn syrup, trans fats, and preservatives. My candies are made from natural ingredients, and one or two pieces will usually satisfy a craving. Raw candy makes a great gift for Halloween, Valentine's Day, and other holidays.

Traditional candy-making is quite technical: you have to melt, temper, and mold the chocolate at just the right temperature or boil the caramel precisely so that it sets properly. Raw candies are quick and easy—made in minutes in a food processor or blender. And Greek Dates (*page 110*) require no machines at all.

CANDY

Truffles, the most admired of chocolate candies, are actually easy to make raw. Boxed in a pretty tin, they're a wonderful gift, especially at holiday time.

dark chocolate truffles

See photo facing page 89.   **YIELD: 24 TRUFFLES**

INGREDIENTS

⅓ cup virgin coconut oil, melted (see page 5)

4 pitted medjool dates

½ cup maple syrup or dark agave syrup

1 cup cocoa powder or raw cacao powder (see page 5)

⅛ teaspoon plus a pinch salt

EQUIPMENT

measuring cups and spoons

small saucepan

2 small mixing bowls

blender

rubber spatula

serving plate

24 (1-inch) **paper or foil candy cups** (optional)

Combine the coconut oil and dates in a small bowl and soak for 30 minutes. Transfer to a blender and add the maple syrup, ¾ cup of the cocoa powder, and all of the salt and process until very smooth. Stop occasionally to scrape down the sides of the blender jar with a rubber spatula. Transfer to a small mixing bowl and chill in the refrigerator for at least 1 hour. Place the remaining ¼ cup cocoa powder in a small bowl and set aside.

Scoop out a heaping ½ teaspoon of the chocolate mixture. Pull it off the measuring spoon with your fingers and lightly roll it into a ball between your palms. Dip and roll the truffle in the cocoa powder, then place it on a plate or in a paper candy cup. Repeat with the remainder of the chocolate mixture. Chill the finished truffles in the refrigerator for at least 1 hour before serving.

Stored in a sealed container in the refrigerator, Chocolate Truffles will keep for 1 week.

COCONUT TRUFFLES: Dip and roll each truffle in unsweetened shredded dried coconut instead of cocoa powder.

CURRY TRUFFLES: Dip and roll each truffle in curry powder instead of cocoa powder.

MEXICAN CHOCOLATE TRUFFLES: Add 1/2 teaspoon of ground cinnamon and a generous pinch of cayenne to the chocolate mixture in the blender. Roll each truffle in cocoa powder.

These are as chewy, sweet, and wonderful as traditional caramels, and much easier to make. Thank you to Cherie Soria, director of Living Light Culinary Institute, for this recipe.

*p*ine nut caramels

YIELD: 36 CARAMELS

INGREDIENTS

1 cup plus 2 tablespoons raw pine nuts

16 pitted medjool dates

½ teaspoon vanilla extract

¼ teaspoon salt

EQUIPMENT

measuring cups and spoons

food processor

medium mixing bowl

36 (1-inch) **paper or foil candy cups** (optional)

Place 1 cup of the pine nuts and all of the dates, vanilla extract, and salt in a food processor fitted with the S blade and process until the mixture begins to stick together. Don't overprocess; a few flecks of pine nuts should still be visible. Transfer the mixture to a medium mixing bowl and place in the freezer for 15 to 30 minutes.

Scoop out 1 teaspoon of the chilled mixture. Pull it off the measuring spoon with your fingers and lightly roll it into a ball between your palms. Press 1 of the reserved pine nuts onto the top of the ball and place the ball on a plate or in a paper candy cup. Repeat with the remaining mixture. Chill for at least 2 hours in the refrigerator or for 1 hour in the freezer. Serve chilled, or straight out of the freezer for a very chewy consistency.

Stored in a sealed container, Pine Nut Caramels will keep for 1 month in the refrigerator or for 3 months in the freezer.

When you feel like going out to buy a candy bar, stop, make this freezer fudge, and vanquish your craving!

carob-cashew freezer fudge

See photo facing page 89.

YIELD: 8 SERVINGS

INGREDIENTS

2 cups raw cashew butter (see page 4)

⅔ cup dark agave syrup or maple syrup

¼ cup raw or roasted carob powder (see page 4)

1 tablespoon virgin coconut oil, melted (see page 5)

2 teaspoons vanilla extract

½ teaspoon salt

½ cup raw cashews (unsoaked), coarsely chopped

EQUIPMENT

measuring cups and spoons

small saucepan

cutting board

chef's knife

food processor

8-inch square glass baking pan

Place the cashew butter, agave syrup, carob powder, coconut oil, vanilla extract, and salt in a food processor and process until smooth. Add the cashews and pulse just until mixed. Press the mixture into an 8-inch glass baking dish. Place in the freezer for at least 2 hours before serving. Cut into squares.

Stored in a sealed container in the freezer, Carob Cashew Freezer Fudge will keep for 3 months.

BLONDIE CASHEW FREEZER FUDGE: Omit the carob powder.

CHOCOLATE CASHEW FREEZER FUDGE: Replace the carob powder with cocoa powder or raw cacao powder (see page 5).

These beautiful treats, made from creamy chocolate, crunchy nuts, and chewy raisins, hold their own with any candy bar.

chocolate candy cups

See photo facing page 89.

YIELD: ABOUT 16 CANDIES

INGREDIENTS

4 pitted large medjool dates

⅓ cup virgin coconut oil, melted (see page 5)

¾ cup cocoa powder or raw cacao powder (see page 5)

½ cup maple syrup or dark agave syrup

⅛ teaspoon plus a pinch salt

2 tablespoons of 2 or more of the following: **sliced raw almonds, chopped raw pistachios, chopped raw pecans, golden raisins, dark raisins, slivered fresh mint, slivered fresh strawberries**

EQUIPMENT

measuring cups and spoons

small saucepan

small mixing bowl

blender

rubber spatula

serving plate

16 (1-inch) **paper or foil candy cups**

Combine the dates and the coconut oil in a small bowl and let soak for 30 minutes. Transfer to a blender and add the cocoa powder, maple syrup, and salt. Process until very smooth, stopping occasionally to scrape down the sides of the blender jar with a rubber spatula.

Place 16 (1-inch) foil baking cups on 2 plates. Fill each cup about three-fourths full with the chocolate mixture. Top each cup with a few of the almonds, pistachios, pecans, raisins, mint, and/or strawberries, pressing them down lightly. Chill the cups in the refrigerator for at least 2 hours before serving. Serve chilled or at room temperature.

Stored in a sealed container in the refrigerator, Chocolate Candy Cups will keep for 2 days.

These make a fine way to finish a Mediterranean meal or to complement a bowl of ice cream or sorbet.

greek dates

See photo facing page 89.   **YIELD: 8 DATES** (4 SERVINGS)

INGREDIENTS

8 pitted medjool dates

2 tablespoons raw walnuts (unsoaked), chopped

2 tablespoons raw almonds (unsoaked), chopped

2 tablespoons dark agave syrup or raw honey (see page 4)

½ teaspoon orange zest (see page 8)

EQUIPMENT

cutting board

chef's knife

measuring spoons

file grater or zester

rubber spatula

Place the walnuts, almonds, agave syrup, and orange zest in a small mixing bowl and stir to combine. Press 1 teaspoon of this nut mixture inside each date and reshape the date around the filling. Chill in the refrigerator for at least 2 hours before serving.

Stored in a sealed container in the refrigerator, Greek Dates will keep for 5 days.

Try this Middle Eastern delicacy as a pick-me-up
with afternoon tea.

chocolate-stuffed dates

YIELD: 8 DATES (4 SERVINGS)

INGREDIENTS

8 pitted medjool dates

**¼ cup Chocolate
Ganache** (page 26),
chilled for at least 1 hour

**8 raw almonds, walnuts,
or pecans** (unsoaked)

EQUIPMENT

measuring spoons

Stuff each date with 1 teaspoon of the ganache and reshape the
date around the filling. Press an almond into the center. Chill
in the refrigerator for at least 2 hours before serving.

Stored in a sealed container in the refrigerator, Chocolate-
Stuffed Dates will keep for 5 days.

ahead of time

Make the Chocolate Ganache and chill it in the refrigerator for
at least 1 hour.

RESOURCES

For more recommendations for raw-food books and websites, visit www.learnrawfood.com.

BOOKS AND VIDEOS

Raw Food Made Easy for 1 or 2 People by Jennifer Cornbleet

www.learnrawfood.com

This book contains my favorite no-cook recipes in quantities ideal for one or two people. Essential time-saving tips and techniques, along with clear instructions, mean that you don't have to toil in the kitchen to enjoy nutritious, delicious raw food.

Raw Food Made Easy (DVD) by Jennifer Cornbleet

www.learnrawfood.com

This DVD expands on the recipes and tips found in my book, *Raw Food Made Easy for 1 or 2 People*.

The Raw Food Revolution Diet by Cherie Soria, Brenda Davis, and Vesanto Melina

www.rawfooddietrevolution.com

Written by renowned raw-food chef Cherie Soria and two dieticians, *The Raw Food Revolution Diet* contains flavorful, satisfying raw-food recipes you can enjoy for a lifetime.

Green Gorilla: The Searchless Raw Diet by Adi Da Samraj

www.dawnhorsepress.org

This book gives simple, practical instructions on how to follow a balanced and effective raw diet. What makes this book unique is Adi Da's wisdom about the significance of the raw diet in the context of spiritual life.

Not-Two Is Peace:
The Ordinary People's Way of Global Cooperative Order by Adi Da Samraj
www.da-peace.org

Here is a passionate call for global change, based on humankind's inherent unity. Especially moving is the author's appeal to stop the exploitation of animals and to go beyond our dependency on meat, for the sake of ourselves and the planet. The entire text of *Not-Two Is Peace*, as well as additional information about the social wisdom of Adi Da, can be found on www.da-peace.org.

WEBSITES

www.learnrawfood.com

My website is the online companion to this book. It provides access to recipes, raw-food ingredients and equipment, newsletters, and upcoming classes and workshops.

www.rawfoodchef.com

Living Light Culinary Arts Institute Cherie Soria and Dan Ladermann, codirectors

This internationally acclaimed raw-food chef school offers certification courses for individuals, chefs, and teachers. It is located in Fort Bragg, California.

www.LapisHolisticHealth.com

Keyvan Golestaneh, practitioner of natural medicine and healer

Visit this website for information about Keyvan Golestaneh's services, including dietary guidance and education.

INDEX

BOOK PUBLISHING COMPANY

since 1974—books that educate, inspire, and empower

To find your favorite vegetarian and alternative health books online,
visit: **www.healthy-eating.com**

*also by
Jennifer
Cornbleet*

Raw Food Made Easy
978-1-57067-173-3
$17.95

Raw Food Made Easy DVD
978-1-57067-203-3
$19.95

Alive in 5 Raw
*Raw Gourmet Meals
in Five Minutes*
Angela Elliott
978-1-57067202-6 $14.95

The Raw Food Revolution Diet
Cherie Soria, Brenda Davis, RD,
Vesanto Melina, MS, RD
978-1-57067-185-2 $21.95

Raw Food Celebrations
Nomi Shannon,
Sheryl Duruz
978-1-57067-228-6
$19.95

Purchase these health titles and cookbooks from your local bookstore
or natural food store, or buy them directly from:

Book Publishing Company • P.O. Box 99 • Summertown, TN 38483 • 1-800-695-2241

Please include $3.95 per book for shipping and handling.